Annotated Constitution of Vanuatu

Annotated Constitution of Vanuatu

David Mossop

Judge of the Supreme Court of the Australian Capital Territory

Preface

The drafting of the Vanuatu Constitution was an impressive achievement of political consensus and of legislative drafting. In the 46 years since Independence the courts of Vanuatu have decided a multitude of constitutional cases. An examination of the constitutional case law of Vanuatu demonstrates the importance of the judicial system to the stability and democratic nature of the government of the country. The Supreme Court and the Court of Appeal have interpreted the Constitution so as "to ensure that it is a clear, workable and practical instrument of the State": *Kilman v Speaker of Parliament of the Republic of Vanuatu* [2011] VUCA 15 at [11].

Given the substantial case law of the Supreme Court and Court of Appeal on the Constitution, the intention of this work was to digest and summarise that case law so as to provide a tool useful to the judiciary and practitioners, rather than providing significant commentary not anchored to the decisions of Vanuatu courts.

It also provides background material relating to the deliberations of the Constitutional Committee which developed the Constitution between April and September 1979, some of which has not been previously publicly available.

I acknowledge the assistance of Tyler O'Hare in identifying and collating constitutional decisions of the Supreme Court and Court of Appeal, Nina Gannon with translation, and Helga Mossop who provided comments on a draft.

I also acknowledge the fundamentally important role played by PacLII (www.paclii.org). The importance of the service provided by PacLII to the countries of the Pacific and to Vanuatu in particular, cannot be overstated. Without the resources available on PacLII a work such as this would be impossible and the administration of justice in Vanuatu and other island nations of the Pacific would be substantially more difficult.

David Mossop
April 2026

Table of Contents

Table of Cases

Introduction

The Constitutional Committee

A Constitutional Committee was established in April 1979 to draft the Constitution for the New Hebrides. The Committee was made up of the Council of Ministers from the New Hebrides Government of National Unity and various representatives of new Hebridean society.[1] It was assisted by Professor Yash Ghai, Professor Charles Zorgbibe, J Aribaud and Bernard Narakobi.

The Committee met between 3 April 1979 and 17 September 1979. There was then a Constitutional Conference on 18 September 1979 which was also attended by representatives of the French and British[2] Governments at which outstanding issues were resolved and the Constitution agreed to. The minutes of the Committee and a collection of the working papers of the Committee was published in 2009. Minutes and working papers of the Committee are also contained in the files of the United Kingdom Foreign and Commonwealth Office.

Independence

The grant of independence to Vanuatu was effected by an exchange of notes between the United Kingdom and France entered into on 23 October 1979.[3] Those notes attached the Constitution in its English and French translations.

Articles 87 (relating to the first Parliament), 93 (relating to the continuation of existing law) and original Article 94 (now deleted) commenced on 23 October 1979. The balance of the provisions of the Constitution commenced on 30 July 1980, the day Vanuatu became independent.

Amendments to the Constitution

The Constitution has been amended on six occasions. The amendments are referred in the annotations to the relevant provisions. A summary of the amendments is as follows.

The Constitution First Amendment Act No 10 of 1980:

(a) changed the name of the country from Republic of the New Hebrides to Republic of Vanuatu;

(b) Amended Article 45 (now Article 47) and 47 (now Article 49) in relation to the appointment of judges and allowed the appointment of acting judges;

---

[1] A list of the members of the Committee and their affiliations is in the Minutes at 9.

[2] Properly described as the Government of the United Kingdom but, as the Constitution refers to "British" laws (Article 95(2)) and the Constitutional Committee referred to the "British Government", "British" is used in this work.

[3] UK Treaty Series No 17 (1980); 1212 UNTS 276.

(c)   Amended article 81 (now Article 83) and 84 (now Article 86) and deleted Article 94 so as to provide for local government councils rather than regional councils.

The Constitution Second Amendment Act No 15 of 1981 amended Article 46 (now Article 48) so as to remove from membership of the Judicial Service Commission "a judge appointed for three years by the President of the Republic".

The Constitution Third Amendment Act No 20 of 1983:

(a)   repealed Article 18 related to the Electoral Commission and substituted Articles 18, 18A (subsequently renumbered as Article 19) and 18B (subsequently renumbered Article 20) which redefined the membership of the Electoral Commission and provided for a Principal Electoral Officer;

(b)   substituted a revised version of Article 35 (now Article 37) which defined the circumstances in which the Speaker of Parliament is entitled to perform the functions of the President.

The Constitution (Fourth Amendment) Act No 20 of 2004 did not come into effect because in *Vohor v Attorney-General* [2004] VUCA 22 it was held that a referendum was required for the amendment to be made. It had proposed amendments requiring a Member of Parliament to vacate his or her seat if the member changed political parties (similar to the changes subsequently made by the eighth amendment), amended the formula in Article 40 that determines the number of Ministers and imposed restrictions on bringing motions of no confidence in the Prime Minister.

The Constitution (Fifth Amendment) Act No 24 of 2006 amended the number of judges (in addition to the Chief Justice) in Article 49(2) from three to "not more than twelve".

The Constitution (Sixth) (Amendment) Act No 27 of 2013:

(a)   amended Articles 4, 5, 10, 13 to allow for the recognition of dual citizenship;

(b)   amended various articles so as to change the references to local government to provincial government;

(c)   amended various articles to change the name of the National Council of Chiefs to the Malvatumauri Council of Chiefs and altered its functions;

(d)   substituted Article 51 so as to limit the power of the Parliament to determine the manner of ascertaining rules of custom relating to land and substituting Article 78 so as to require the Parliament to formalise the recognition of customary institutions to resolve land ownership or disputes over land.

The Constitution (Seventh) Amendment Act No 1 of 2019 did not come into effect because in *Saemon v Tallis* [2019] VUCA 44 it was held that a referendum was required for the amendment to be made. It had proposed a new Article 46A allowing the appointment of Parliamentary Secretaries from among the Members of Parliament, and their removal.

The Constitution (Eighth) (Amendment) Act No 21 of 2023:

(a) inserted Article 17A which has the effect of declaring the seat of a member of Parliament vacant if the member, having been a candidate of a political party, resigns from the party or is terminated as a member of that party;

(b) inserted Article 17B requiring members of Parliament elected as an independent, the sole representative of a party or a representative of a custom movement to declare his or her affiliation with a political party within three months of the first sitting of Parliament or have the seat declared vacant.

On 7 May 2025 a bill for the Constitution (Ninth) (Amendment) Act No 7 of 2025 was passed. If it enters into force, it would incorporate a 12-month grace period, free of no confidence votes, for a new Prime Minister and added laws for the purpose of "economic development zones" as an exception to the requirement for equal treatment under Article 5(1)(k) of the Constitution. The bill was the subject of *President of the Republic of Vanuatu v Speaker of Parliament* [2025] VUSC 286 in which the Supreme Court did not find that it was inconsistent with the Constitution. It requires a referendum under Article 86 of the Constitution before it can come into effect.

Article numbers in the Constitution

As a result of the Constitution Third Amendment Act 1983, two new sections were added to the Constitution (Articles 18A and 18B). When the 1988 consolidation of laws was prepared under the Revision and Consolidation of the Laws Act [CAP 185], the sections were renumbered 19 and 20 with the effect that all subsequent Articles in the Constitution were required to be renumbered. Therefore references to article numbers greater than Article 18 at the time of Independence will be different to those presently in effect. Given that the case law predominantly post-dates the renumbering, it is convenient to refer to the articles based upon their current numbering rather than noting, in relation to each article after Article 18, the change in the numbering.

Version of the Constitution

This annotated Constitution is based upon the Consolidated English version of the Constitution as at 29 April 2020 obtained from parliament.gov.vu in 2025. That version consolidates the amendments made by Act 10 of 1980, Act 15 of 1981, Act 20 of 1983, Act 24 of 2006 and Act 27 of 2013. The amendments made by Act 21 of 2023 have been manually incorporated into that version.

Citations

Cases are cited using the medium neutral citations available on PacLII (www.paclii.org). Where the original judgment uses numbered paragraphs the relevant paragraph is referred to in square brackets (for example *Republic of Vanuatu v Benard* [2016] VUCA 4 at [20]). Where the original judgment did not use numbered paragraphs, the relevant page of the original decision is referred to (for example *Attorney-General v Jimmy* [1996] VUCA 1 at 8). Where the original decision that would indicate either page numbers or paragraph numbers is not available (ie there is only an html version on PacLII), no pinpoint reference is given.

Where there are medium neutral citations, VUSC or VUCA, on PacLII and the decision is also reported in the Vanuatu Law Reports, only the medium neutral citation is used. However where the case does not have a VUSC or VUCA citation then the Vanuatu Law Reports citation (Van LR) and the citation given by PacLII (VULawRp) are both provided. That is because, in contrast to the Van LR citation, which simply identifies that the decision was given between 1980 and 1994, the VULawRp citation immediately identifies the individual year in which the judgment was delivered and this may be useful in understanding the significance of the decision. As original page numbers are not available for these reports, pinpoint citations are given based upon the pagination of the downloadable version of the judgment on PacLII.

Case names generally follow those used on PacLII. In a small number of cases, case names have been changed to correct an error. Further, case names have been simplified by:

(a)   the removal of "The" from the name of a party where it is unnecessary (for example, "Republic of Vanuatu" rather than "The Republic of Vanuatu").

(b)   the removal of "In re the Constitution" or similar where the names of the parties are given as well (for example "Nixon v Republic of Vanuatu" rather than "In re the Constitution, Nixon v Republic of Vanuatu").

Sources of extrinsic materials

A collection of the minutes of the Constitutional Committee which met between April and September 1979 and its working papers entitled *Constitutional Committee = Comite Constitutionnel: Ripablik blong Vanuatu, Epril - Septemba 1979* was obtained from the Vanuatu Constitutional Archive on PacLII: www.paclii.org/countries/vu/legis/const_archive. In footnotes, this collection of minutes and working papers is cited as "Minutes" with the relevant page number.

The files of the United Kingdom Foreign and Commonwealth Office relevant to the deliberations of the Constitutional Committee and the preparation for independence have also been relied upon. These bear file numbers FCO107/106, FCO107/107, FCO107/108, FCO107/109, FCO107/111. They are held by the National Archives of the United Kingdom (www.nationalarchives.gov.uk). In footnotes, the Foreign and Commonwealth Office files are referred to by their file numbers.

These two sources provide access to all of the minutes of the Constitutional Committee and the large majority of the Committee's working papers. A table identifying where relevant working papers may be located is included at page 153 below.

Abbreviated references to sources

Sources are referred to in the text using abbreviations as follow.

PV: Proces verbeaux (French for "minutes"), the minutes of the Constitutional Committee. These are numbered PV1 to PV50 and PV52. The minutes of the Constitutional Conference held on 18 September 1979 are PV51. It is this collection of minutes which is the source of information about the discussions of the Committee and the Conference.

Minutes: References to Minutes is a reference to the publication *Constitutional Committee = Comite Constitutionnel: Ripablik blong Vanuatu, Epril - Septemba 1979* (see "Sources of Extrinsic Materials" above). When referring to the Minutes of the Constitutional Committee a reference to the PV number (including a relevant paragraph reference) will also be included.

Working papers of the Constitutional Committee: These are referred to by reference to the letter and number given to them by the Committee. They reflect drafts of proposed constitutional provisions and hence disclose the evolution of those provisions during the deliberations of the Committee. Each different topic that needed to be addressed was given a letter, A to R. Papers addressing issues relevant to that topic were then sequentially numbered (for example A1, A2 etc). Where revisions were made on a particular issue those where then sequentially numbered (for example A2(2), A2(3)). A table of the working papers and where they may be found is at page 153 below.

Foreign and Commonwealth Office files: Where files of the United Kingdom Foreign and Commonwealth Office are referred to (see "Sources of Extrinsic Materials" above) they are referred to by their file number, for example FCO107/108. In most cases the working papers found in these files are also reproduced in the Minutes. Where that is the case both references are given. However where a document only appears in the files, the file reference alone is given.

CONSTITUTION OF THE REPUBLIC OF VANUATU
ARRANGEMENT OF ARTICLES

CHAPTER 13 – DECENTRALISATION

CHAPTER 14 – AMENDMENT OF THE CONSTITUTION

CHAPTER 15 – TRANSITIONAL PROVISIONS

CONSTITUTION OF THE REPUBLIC OF VANUATU

WE, the people of Vanuatu,

PROUD of our struggle for freedom,

DETERMINED to safeguard the achievements of this struggle,

CHERISHING our ethnic, linguistic and cultural diversity,

MINDFUL at the same time of our common destiny,

HEREBY proclaim the establishment of the united and free Republic of Vanuatu founded on traditional Melanesian values, faith in God, and Christian principles,

AND for this purpose give ourselves this Constitution.

Constitutional Committee

Various draft preambles were put forward during the deliberations of the Constitutional Committee.[4] The issue was principally discussed on 13 September 1979.[5] A further draft preamble had been prepared by Professor Ghai and J Aribaud with the help of the Steering Committee. This draft formed the basis of the preamble that was adopted.[6]

A number of amendments were proposed or made to the draft. A proposal was put forward to insert "good" or "positive" before "traditional Melanesian values" (sorcery being the example given of a "bad" Melanesian tradition) but this was not adopted, the comment being made that "the Constitution, especially in the chapter on human rights, provided protection against the worse aspects of Melanesian traditions".[7] The words "faith in God" were inserted between "Melanesian values" and "Christian principles".[8] The word "achievements" was substituted for "fruits" that had appeared in the draft.[9]

Commentary

Status of the Preamble

The Preamble is a part of the Constitution. However, it has no more than an interpretive role. It is distinct from the regular machinery of the Constitution and should not be ascribed the same effect as an operative provision: *President of the Republic of Vanuatu v Speaker of Parliament* [2008] VUSC 77 at 14-15. The Preamble

---

[4] See Minutes 63, 64 (PV22), 122 (PV39), 157-159 (PV47), 231, working paper G7 (Minutes 242), working paper G8 (Minutes 243), working paper G9 (FCO107/108).

[5] Minutes 157-159 (PV47[4]-[26]).

[6] Working paper G9: FCO107/108.

[7] Minutes 158 (PV47[18]-[20]).

[8] Minutes 158 (PV47[21]).

[9] Minutes 158 (PV47[22]).

may be used to interpret other provisions of the Constitution which are ambiguous: *President of the Republic of Vanuatu v Speaker of Parliament* [2008] VUSC 77 at 15, 28. The terms of the Preamble do not, of themselves, create a legal principle which a bill may be found to be inconsistent with under Article 16(4): *President of the Republic of Vanuatu v Speaker of Parliament* [2008] VUSC 77 at 18.

Approach to interpretation of the Constitution

The Constitution is to be given "a fair, large and liberal interpretation": *Stage Four Ltd v Proprietors of Strata Plan 0011* [2023] VUCA 36 at [14].

As the supreme law of the land, the Constitution must not be treated as an Act of Parliament but as *sui generis* calling for principles of interpretation of its own: *Kilman v Speaker of Parliament of the Republic of Vanuatu* [2011] VUCA 15 at [10]-[11]; *Silas v Public Service Commission* [2014] VUCA 9 at [20]; *Kilbride Ltd v Republic of Vanuatu* [2020] VUCA 24 at [7]; *President of the Republic of Vanuatu v Speaker of the Parliament* [2023] VUSC 33 at [18].

In *Virelala v Ombudsman* [1997] VUSC 35 at 20-25 Lunabek ACJ outlined his approach to the interpretation of the Constitution, comparing it to and contrasting it with the constitutions of Papua New Guinea and Australia. In *President of the Republic of Vanuatu v Speaker of the Parliament* [2023] VUSC 33 at [34] he summarised his approach as follows:

> The Constitution is to be interpreted and applied by keeping in mind and be in line with the progress of the country, and adapt themselves to the new developments of times and circumstances. The powers and related provisions in the Constitution must be read in an organic, developing or progressive manner.

In *Virelala* he identified (at 23-24) that an Act or a provision of an Act would be declared to be unconstitutional when it infringed one of the fundamental rights and freedoms guaranteed and protected under Article 5 of the Constitution or where "there is an express or explicit prohibition provision contained in the Constitution to do or not to do something, but Parliament, nevertheless, legislates to that prohibited effect in contravention of the constitutional express prohibition provision".

In *Wells v Taga Tarikarea* [2003] VUSC 103 at 2-3 Lunabek CJ explained his approach to interpreting the Constitution, referring to decisions of the Supreme Courts of Canada and the United States which emphasised that the Constitution must be capable of "growth and development over time to meet new social political and historical realities often unimagined by its framers" and be understood as a "continuing instrument of government".

In *Kilman v Attorney-General* [1997] VUSC 3 at 6 the Lunabek ACJ said:

> The Court when interpreting the Constitution must adopt a broad-oriented and purposive approach directed towards advancing the Constitutional objectives taking due account to the country circumstances *and resources*. (Emphasis added)

Where there is room for debate or possible ambiguity, assistance may be gained from a consideration of the way parliaments in other places have operated in the past or operate now but that is subject to the clear and unambiguous words of the Constitution which is the supreme law: *Tari v Natapei* [2001] VUCA 18 at 3.

In *Vohor v Attorney-General* [2004] VUCA 22, reliance was placed in submissions upon certain of the minutes of the Constitutional Committee for the purpose of interpreting the scope of Article 86. The Court of Appeal said (at [18]) that these were of "no assistance to the Court as they relate to beliefs or feelings of the members of the committee and we are not referred to the final recommendation of the committee".

Interpretation Act not applicable

The terms of the Constitution should not be interpreted by reference to the Interpretation Act: *Silas v Public Service Commission* [2014] VUCA 9 at [20]; *President of the Republic of Vanuatu v Speaker of the Parliament* [2023] VUSC 33 at [32].

CHAPTER 1 – THE STATE AND SOVEREIGNTY

Constitutional Committee

Two working papers were prepared relevant to this chapter.[10] The principal discussion of the articles in this Chapter occurred on 23 and 24 July 1979.[11]

1. Republic of Vanuatu

The Republic of Vanuatu is a sovereign democratic state.

Constitutional Committee

In response to a submission from the New Hebrides Christian Council,[12] there was discussion on 23 and 24 July 1979 of whether there should be a reference to Christianity or Melanesian values in the part of the Constitution dealing with sovereignty.[13] After considerable discussion it was decided that Professors Zorgbibe and Ghai would draft a preamble in which the question of religious faith and custom would be covered[14] and this was the course ultimately adopted.

Amendments

The Constitution First Amendment Act No 10 of 1980 amended the name of the country in Article 1 and other Articles of the Constitution from the New Hebrides to Vanuatu. It also changed the references to "New Hebridean" in the Constitution to "Ni-Vanuatu".

2. Constitution supreme law

The Constitution is the supreme law of the Republic of Vanuatu.

Commentary

Function of the Supreme Court in relation to the Constitution

In *Vanuaroroa v Natapei* [2011] VUSC 92 at 15 the Supreme Court explained its function in relation to the Constitution as follows:

> It is the function and duty of the Supreme Court to vindicate the supremacy of the Constitution so as to ensure that the rule of law is maintained at all times in this Republic and particularly more so when the Constitution, the parliamentary democratic system of government, the fundamental rights guaranteed under it, the fundamental institutions of the government created by the Constitution and the principles of their operations and interrelations are not understood by the

---

[10] Working papers R1 (FCO107/107) and R1(2) (FCO107/108).

[11] Minutes 60-63 (PV21, PV22).

[12] The submission contained draft constitutional provisions and is reproduced in Minutes 196-198.

[13] Minutes 60-63 (PV21, PV22).

[14] Minutes 63 (PV22[9]).

majority of the people of Vanuatu as they are not part of their cultures and traditions but they must respect and obey the Constitution as the supreme law of Vanuatu.

Inconsistency with the Constitution

The Supreme Court has power to strike down as invalid any legislation infringing the Constitution: *Stage Four Ltd v Proprietors of Strata Plan 0011* [2023] VUCA 36 at [14].

The power of the Supreme Court to declare a statutory provision invalid does not extend to requiring it to be struck out or removed: see *Wu Kim Ming v Republic of Vanuatu* [2021] VUSC 29 at [116] and the cases there cited. It has been suggested that a different approach may be possible where there is a reference to the Court by the President under Article 16(4), where advice may include excising words: *Attorney-General v Timakata* [1993] VUCA 2 at 8; *Wu Kim Ming* at [118].

In *Ombudsman v Batick* [2001] VUSC 45 at 20 the Supreme Court adopted a test which indicated that an Act will be inconsistent with the Constitution if:

(a)   it directly collides with the Constitution so that it is impossible to follow both the Constitution and the Act;

(b)   the Constitution evinces an intention to be exhaustive on the subject covered by the Act.

Reading down of inconsistent Acts

Section 9(1) of the Interpretation Act [CAP 132] requires that "Every Act shall be read and construed subject to the Constitution and where any provision of an Act conflicts with a provision of the Constitution the latter provision shall prevail." Section 9(2) permits reading down of provisions which conflict with the Constitution, providing: "Where a provision in an Act conflicts with a provision in the Constitution the Act shall nevertheless be valid to the extent that it is not in conflict with the Constitution." Section 9 applies to subordinate legislation and statutory instruments: see Interpretation Act ss 1, 12.

Examples of reading down

In *Wu Kim Ming v Republic of Vanuatu* [2021] VUSC 29 provisions of the *Land Leases Act* inserted by the *Land Leases Amendment Act* No 35 of 2014 were found to amount to unjustified deprivation of property contrary to Article 5(1)(j) of the Constitution insofar as they applied in relation to leases entered into prior to their commencement: at [110], [126],[130]. However by operation of s 9(2) of the Interpretation Act they were interpreted as only applying to leases entered into after the commencement of the amending Act: at [111], [126], [130]-[131].

---

3. National and official languages

(1)   The national language of the Republic of Vanuatu is Bislama. The official languages are Bislama, English and French. The principal languages of education are English and French.

(2)   The Republic of Vanuatu shall protect the different local languages which are part of the national heritage, and may declare one of them as a national language.

Constitutional Committee

On 17 April 1979 there was debate as to whether there should be any official language and whether French and English should be kept. Professor Zorgbibe suggested a possible solution was for Bislama to be designated the "national language – thereby indicating the New Hebrides' cultural identity – and for French and English to be official languages".[15] This proposal was repeated on 23 July 1979.[16] The minutes of the meeting on 23 July 1979 record:[17]

> Prof Zorgbibe explained that by "national" language, he meant the language that was the cultural expression of the country; by "official" languages, he meant working languages and languages used for external communications. He appreciated that having two official languages could be costly, but he also pointed out that this could be an asset within the context of the Pacific.

The terms ultimately agreed to by the Committee were: "The national language of the New Hebrides is Bislama. The working languages of the New Hebrides are French, English and Bislama. The Republic will protect the existence of the various local languages which are part of the cultural wealth of the nation and may raise one of these languages to the status of national language".[18]

The Minutes do not disclose how the proposed article was amended so that it instead made reference to the "principal languages of education" as appears in Article 3. At the last meeting of the Committee on 17 September 1979 there was some discussion of the need to hear linguists in relation to Article 3 although it was provisionally adopted and the issue was not returned to.[19]

---

[15]   Minutes 26 (PV6[6]).
[16]   Minutes 60 (PV21[2]).
[17]   Minutes 61 (PV21[10]).
[18]   Minutes 61 (PV21[13]).
[19]   Minutes 174-175 (PV50[35]).

> ## 4. National sovereignty, the electoral franchise and political parties
>
> (1) National sovereignty belongs to the people of Vanuatu which they exercise through their elected representatives.
>
> (2) The franchise is universal, equal and secret. Subject to such conditions or restrictions as may be prescribed by Parliament, every citizen of Vanuatu who is at least 18 years of age shall be entitled to vote.
>
> (3) Subject to any restrictions imposed by law, political parties may be formed freely and may contest elections. They shall respect the Constitution and the principles of democracy.
>
> (4) For the purposes of determining national sovereignty, "people of Vanuatu" means all indigenous and naturalised citizens of Vanuatu.

Constitutional Committee

The words "Subject to such conditions or restrictions as may be prescribed by Parliament" which now form the opening words of the second sentence of Article 4(2) were not included in either of the working papers put before the Committee.[20] They had been tentatively included when the Constitution as a whole was revised by the legal draftsman and their inclusion was approved on 17 September 1979, the last meeting of the Committee before the Constitutional Conference.[21]

Amendments

Article 4(4) was inserted by the Constitution (Sixth) (Amendment) Act No 27 of 2013.

The Constitution (Eighth) (Amendment) Act No 21 of 2023 inserted at the beginning of Article 4(3) the words "Subject to any restrictions imposed by law". That Act also inserted Articles 17A and 17B.

Commentary

Article 4(2)

The eligibility criteria in s 24 of the Representation of the People Act [CAP 146] are conditions or restrictions prescribed by Parliament for the purposes of Article 4(2): *Vinbel v Asang* [2023] VUSC 38.

Article 4(2) is relevant only to voting in elections for the Parliament. It does not confer rights in relation to municipal elections: *Vire v Republic of Vanuatu* [2009] VUSC 115 at 5.

---

[20] Working papers R1 (FCO107/107) and R1(2) (FCO107/108).

[21] Minutes 174 (PV50[30]).

Article 4(2) is not contravened by requiring citizens to vote in the electorate where they are resident: *Tonge v Republic of Vanuatu* [2007] VUSC 5 at 9-10.

Article 4(3)

The right to form political parties under Article 4(3) does not extend to a right to use a party name, slogan or logo which would constitute passing off at common law: *Salwai v The Union of Moderate Patis Committee (Inc)* [2012] VUCA 19 at [45]-[48].

CHAPTER 2 – FUNDAMENTAL RIGHTS AND DUTIES

PART I – Fundamental Rights

5. Fundamental rights and freedoms of the individual

(1) The Republic of Vanuatu recognises, that, subject to any restrictions imposed by law on non-citizens and holders of dual citizenship who are not indigenous or naturalised citizens, all persons are entitled to the following fundamental rights and freedoms of the individual without discrimination on the grounds of race, place of origin, religious or traditional beliefs, political opinions, language or sex but subject to respect for the rights and freedoms of others and to the legitimate public interest in defence, safety, public order, welfare and health –

(a) life;

(b) liberty;

(c) security of the person;

(d) protection of the law;

(e) freedom from inhuman treatment and forced labour;

(f) freedom of conscience and worship;

(g) freedom of expression;

(h) freedom of assembly and association;

(i) freedom of movement;

(j) protection for the privacy of the home and other property and from unjust deprivation of property;

(k) equal treatment under the law or administrative action, except that no law shall be inconsistent with this sub-paragraph insofar as it makes provision for the special benefit, welfare, protection or advancement of females, children and young persons, members of under-privileged groups or inhabitants of less developed areas.

(2) Protection of the law shall include the following –

(a) everyone charged with an offence shall have a fair hearing, within a reasonable time, by an independent and impartial court and be afforded a lawyer if it is a serious offence;

(b) everyone is presumed innocent until a court establishes his guilt according to law;

<table>
<tr><td>(c)</td><td>everyone charged shall be informed promptly in a language he understands of the offence with which he is being charged;</td></tr>
<tr><td>(d)</td><td>if an accused does not understand the language to be used in the proceedings he shall be provided with an interpreter throughout the proceedings;</td></tr>
<tr><td>(e)</td><td>a person shall not be tried in his absence without his consent unless he makes it impossible for the court to proceed in his presence;</td></tr>
<tr><td>(f)</td><td>no-one shall be convicted in respect of an act or omission which did not constitute an offence known to written or custom law at the time it was committed;</td></tr>
<tr><td>(g)</td><td>no-one shall be punished with a greater penalty than that which exists at the time of the commission of the offence;</td></tr>
<tr><td>(h)</td><td>no person who has been pardoned, or tried and convicted or acquitted, shall be tried again for the same offence or any other offence of which he could have been convicted at his trial.</td></tr>
</table>

Constitutional Committee

A statement of fundamental rights and their enforcement by an independent judiciary were identified as among the most important issues to be determined by the Committee at its first meeting.[22] Professor Ghai's original proposal[23] contained three clauses each containing an aggregation of rights. It included a provision for enforcement of the rights by the Supreme Court which Professor Zorgbibe described as "inspired by a British-style system with a Supreme Court able to give injunctions etc to protect those rights".[24] Concerns were expressed about the extent of freedom of religion and "the activity of new religions or sects implanting themselves".[25] The provisions relating to fundamental rights were discussed on 17 April[26], 24 July[27] and 11 August 1979.[28]

The words "or traditional" in the chapeau to Article 5(1) were inserted at the suggestion of Professor Zorgbibe.[29] His suggestion that the rights to freedom of movement be qualified by the words "within the limits set by local custom"[30] was not taken up.

---

22 Minutes 13 (PV1).
23 Working paper G2: FCO107/107.
24 Minutes 27 (PV6[8]).
25 Minutes 27 (PV6[10]).
26 Minutes 27 (PV6).
27 Minutes 63-64 (PV22[12]-[16]).
28 Minutes 111 (PV35[21]-[25]).
29 Minutes 63 (PV22[12]).
30 Minutes 63 (PV22[12]).

The working paper approved on 11 August 1979[31] included a provision qualifying the freedom of conscience and worship by providing a limit on unsolicited or uninvited intervention into the religious affairs of another:[32]

> The freedom of conscience and worship may be qualified as follows-
>
> (i) No person is entitled to intervene or enter unsolicited or uninvited into the religious affairs of another or into an area already served by a religion, without:
>
> a) the express request of the local community in which a person is to practice his religion;
>
> b) and the approval of the Minister responsible for religious affairs.

This was included at the request of the New Hebrides Christian Council. Notwithstanding the Committee's approval of the working paper, it appears to have been removed following a discussion at the last meeting of the Constitutional Committee before the Constitutional Conference where it was proposed "to leave any restriction of this freedom to an organic law, if Parliament felt such a restriction to be necessary" although a specific decision of the Committee is not recorded in the Minutes.[33]

Amendments

In Article 5(1) the words "and holders of dual citizenship who are not indigenous or naturalised citizens" were inserted by the Constitution (Sixth) (Amendment) Act No 27 of 2013.

Commentary

Article 5(1) chapeau

The chapeau of Article 5 identifies three sources of restrictions upon the rights in the Article. They are:

(a)   any restrictions imposed by law on noncitizens and holders of dual citizenship who are not indigenous or naturalised citizens;

(b)   the rights are subject to respect for the rights and freedoms of others; and

(c)   the rights are subject to the legitimate public interest in defence, safety, public order, welfare and health.

Each of these contains a potential qualification upon the extent to which the rights articulated in Article 5 may be able to be enforced under Article 6.

Article 5(1) chapeau: non-citizens

The recognition of rights in Article 5(1) is "subject to any restrictions imposed by law on non-citizens and holders of dual citizenship who are not indigenous or

---

[31] Working paper G6: Minutes 240-241; FCO107/108.
[32] Minutes 241; FCO107/108.
[33] Minutes 175 (PV50[37]-[42]).

naturalised citizens". Such restrictions must be "imposed by law" and any restrictions on non-citizens must "apply specifically to non-citizens": *Ayamiseba v Attorney-General* [2006] VUSC 21 at [83]. As a consequence a provision of the Immigration Act [CAP 66] which permitted removal of a non-citizen without prior notice was held to be valid in *Ayamiseba*.

The effect of the decision in *Ayamiseba* is that non-citzens (and the other persons referred to in the chapeau) will have all of the rights in Article 5(1) unless there is a law that specifically applies to them.

An injunction granted by a court against a non-citizen was found to be a restriction imposed by law for the purposes of the chapeau to Article 5 in *Daniel v D'Imecourt* [1998] VUSC 9.

Article 5(1) chapeau: rights and freedoms of others

In relation to the operation of time limits for the bringing of proceedings, in *Rombu v Family Rasu* [2006] VUCA 22 at 4 the Court of Appeal said:

> A second observation is that the fundamental rights and freedoms recognised in Article 5(1) of the Constitution are "subject to respect for the rights and freedoms of others and to the legitimate public interest in defence, safety, public order, welfare and health." In balancing the rights of parties the importance of achieving certainty for those who are parties to a dispute, and the importance in the public interest of bringing disputes to finality are factors that must be brought into account. These considerations provide the justification for imposing limitation periods on the enforcement of rights, and must be taken into account in considering the reasonableness of the requirements of s 22 of the Island Courts Act.

Article 5(1) chapeau: legitimate public interests

The rights in Article 5(1) are "subject to respect for the rights and freedoms of others and to the legitimate public interest in defence, safety, public order, welfare and health".

In determining where the public interest lies the Parliament must be allowed a "wide margin of appreciation": *Groupe Nairobi (Vanuatu) Ltd v Government of the Republic of Vanuatu* [2009] VUCA 35 at 15; *Stage Four Ltd v Proprietors of Strata Plan 0011* [2023] VUCA 36 at [43].

Whether or not the acquisition of land for the purpose of "green space" was within the scope of "defence, safety, public order, welfare and health" was raised but not determined in *Kilbride Ltd v Republic of Vanuatu* [2020] VUCA 24. The Court said at [40]:

> However we note that Article 5, like the Constitution generally, must be given a generous interpretation that best suits the intended purpose of the paramount law, and the words of the proviso should be understood generally as indicative of the many aspects of public administration which Parliament must regulate.

Terra Holdings Ltd v Sope [2012] VUCA 16 involved a proposal to reclaim land below the low water mark. The Court found that the deprivation of the custom owner's property was not within the proviso in Article 5(1). The Court said (at [60]) that "a degree of latitude must be allowed to the Government to decide what is in the public interest" but did not agree that "advancing tourism" was "a public interest in defence, safety, public order, welfare and health". It therefore found that the deprivation of property would be "unjust" for the purposes of Article 5(1)(a).

Article 5 provides rights against the government

The rights in Article 5 are rights that persons have in relation to the government of Vanuatu as distinct from rights against private persons. In *Mass v Government of the Republic of Vanuatu* [2018] VUCA 11 at [40]-[41] the Court of Appeal said:

> 40. The formulation of the appellant's claims and the particulars in this category of situations fails to recognize and reflect that the constitutional obligations to recognize and respect guaranteed fundamental rights and freedoms is an obligation imposed on public officers as part of the public law of the Republic. In particular the application fails to recognize that constitutional rights and freedoms arising under Article 5 are not infringed by wrongful conduct of individuals who are not public officers. The constitutional duty to recognize Article 5 rights and freedoms is imposed on public officers whilst, and only whilst they are exercising those functions. In François v Ozols [1998] VUCA 5 this court noted that the opening words of Article 5 are critical to the understanding of the nature of the fundamental rights and freedoms which it guaranteed. The court said the words: "The Republic of Vanuatu recognizes" ... are not apt to create new private rights and obligations between individuals. The words are a covenant by the Republic to all persons (subject only to a qualification in respect of non-citizens) that in each relationship with them the Republic will recognize the fundamental rights and freedoms set out in Article 5".

> 41. The obligations recognized in Article 5 do not alter the general law which governs the relationship of citizens among themselves. For example, if one citizen deprives another of property, Article 5(g) does not enable the deprived citizen to seek constitutional redress. The only available remedy is for the deprived citizen to seek damages under the general law.

If a constitutional petition names as a respondent someone who is a private individual and not a government official this is likely to be an indication that the petition is misconceived and that it seeks to complain about infringement of rights which are not rights and freedoms of the kind protected by Article 5: *Francois v Ozols* [1998] VUCA 5 at 11.

Government liability for public officials

Where there is a question for the purposes of constitutional redress whether the Republic is responsible for the conduct of a public officer, the test to be applied is that in *Temar v Government of the Republic of Vanuatu* [2005] VUCA 30: *Mass v Government of the Republic of Vanuatu* [2018] VUCA 11 at [46]. That involves asking whether the unauthorised and wrongful act of the servant is not so connected with the authorised act as to be a mode of doing it but is an independent act for which the master is not responsible, because the servant is not acting in the course of his employment but has gone outside it: *Mass* at [43].

The Republic will be liable for breaches of fundamental rights committed by police even though in proceedings in tort the government would not be liable for the tortious actions of such police because of their status as officers rather than employees: *Iaukas v Republic of Vanuatu* [2015] VUSC 131 at [38]-[51].

Article 5(1)(d): protection of the law

Relationship to Article 5(2)

The content of Article 5(1)(d) is elaborated upon in Article 5(2). However Article 5(2) is an inclusive statement of what protection of the law involves and the content of Article 5(1)(d) is not confined by Article 5(2): *Kalnpel v Government of the Republic of Vanuatu* [2023] VUCA 10 at [25].

In *Kalo v Public Service Commission (No 1)* (1987) VULawRp 7; [1980-1994] Van LR 305 at 8 the Supreme Court found that Article 5(2)(a)-(e) can apply to either a civil or a criminal matter but (f)-(h) apply to criminal matters alone.

Natural justice

In *Attorney-General v Timakata* [1993] VUCA 2 at 4 the Court of Appeal explained the scope of Article 5(1)(d) saying:

> The provisions of the Article 5 of the Constitution must be given a generous interpretation: See Ong Ah Chuan v Public Prosecutor [1981] AC 648 at 670. Clearly a right to the protection of the law must include a right to invoke the jurisdiction of the Courts to enforce the rights of the citizen. There is no justification for restricting the Constitutional provision so that it ensures that a citizen may approach the Courts to seek the protection only of rights conferred by the Constitution; the protection of the law extends to all rights conferred by the law. The Parliament has power subject to the Constitution to take away or modify rights but while a right exists the citizen may apply to the Courts to protect it. However the right to the protection of the law given by Article 5(1)(d) is wider than a right to seek legal redress. The decision of the Privy Council in Ong Ah Chuan v Public Prosecutor provides useful guidance as to the meaning of the words "protection of the law" in Article 5(1)(d).

> ...

> It appears from that decision that a provision such as article 5(1)(d) not only prevents the Parliament from ousting the jurisdiction of the Courts but also prevents the Parliament from abrogating those principles of natural justice which may rightly be regarded as fundamental. That does not mean that all the rules which governed the exercise of administrative functions at the date of the commencement of the Constitution are necessarily preserved forever. Subject of course to the Constitution, the Parliament of Vanuatu is given plenary powers by article 16(1) of the Constitution and in the exercise of those powers it may repeal or alter existing law: See article 95 of the Constitution. Article 5(1)(d) prevents the

Parliament from altering only those rules of natural justice which are truly fundamental.

Also in *Timakata* the Court

(a)   (at 3) made it clear that the elaboration on Article 5(1)(d) in Article 5(2) was not exhaustive, saying: "Sub-article 5(2) of the Constitution states that the protection of the law shall include certain specified rights in criminal matters, but that provision is clearly not exhaustive";

(b)   (at 7) said that the rules of natural justice do not indicate that a failure to give reasons is a denial of the protection guaranteed by Article 5(1)(a);

(c)   (at 7) found that a statutory duty to refuse reasons for refusal or revocation of a licence upon which the livelihood of a citizen depends was a breach of Article 5(1)(d);

(d)   (at 8) left open the question as to whether under Article 16(4) it is open to the Supreme Court to advise the President to assent to the remainder of a bill after excising the words which give rise to the inconsistency with the Constitution.

In *Public Service Commission v Willie* [1993] VUCA 1 at 5 the Court of Appeal said "The rules of natural justice are not standardised but depend on all the circumstances of any particular case…"

In *Boulekone v Timakata* [1986] VULawRp 13; [1980-1994] Van LR 228 at 2 the Court of Appeal said:

> Fundamental rights are set out in Article 5(1) which includes under paragraph (d) 'protection of the law'. Article 5(2) describes what is meant by 'protection of the law'. Without repeating it in detail one can say that it specifies the essential requirements of a fair hearing by anyone facing an allegation, that is to say, the principles of natural justice as known and understood in the free and democratic world will be applied by the tribunal considering the allegation. All Tribunals in Vanuatu are accordingly bound by the rules of natural justice whether they be administrative in function or purely judicial.

This involves an expansion of the entitlement in Article 5(2)(a) which refers to the entitlement to a fair hearing for "everyone charged with an offence" because the judgment refers to all tribunals whether they are administrative or judicial in function. See also *Kalsakau v Public Service Commission of the Republic of Vanuatu* [1994] VUSC 10 at 4-5.

The right in Article 5(1)(d) to protection of the law has been said to incorporate "the common law principle of natural justice and fairness": *Ayamiseba v Attorney-General* [2006] VUSC 21 at [102]. The reference to "fairness" in that case should be understood as "procedural fairness" rather than any concept of substantive fairness, as the latter is not a requirement of the common law referred to in this decision. There are some authorities that make reference to Article 5(1)(d) as being a guarantee of both procedural fairness and "substantive justice", for example, *Malifa v Attorney-General* [1999] VUSC 43 at 14-15. A breach of procedural fairness was found to give rise to a breach of Article 5(1)(d) and an entitlement to relief in *Vanva v Minister of Internal Affairs* [2002] VUSC 54.

In *Kuatpen v Lal* [2025] VUCA 18 at [20] the Court of Appeal referred to the fact that Article 5(1)(d) "incorporates the fundamental rules of natural justice that [are] part and parcel of the common law" and also (at [26]-[29]) to cases in which "the procedure set down by legislation is so detailed that there is no room for the rules of natural justice to be implied". The Court of Appeal did not describe how such cases fitted within Article 5(1)(d).

Exclusion of judicial review

A statutory provision which provided that a decision of the Electoral Commission "shall not be questioned in any court" constitutes a denial of the protection of the law afforded by Article 5(1)(d) and is void and of no effect: *Masdan v Electoral Commission* [2002] VUSC 22.

In *Yoon v Republic of Vanuatu* [2023] VUSC 239 at [20] the Supreme Court held that if a statutory provision had been interpreted as permitting removal of a person from Vanuatu that would have removed the right of the subject to review by the Supreme Court and would have been unconstitutional as it involved a breach of Article 5(1)(d). The statutory provision was not so interpreted and hence was not unconstitutional.

Application of Article 5(1)(d) to court decisions

While the striking out of a claim is not inherently contrary to Article 5(1)(d), the court must nevertheless be cautious to ensure its exercise of discretion does not violate that guarantee: *Hungtali v Kalo* [2024] VUSC 136 at [15]. If the pleading raises a serious contested issue then it should not be struck out and it should should be determined after a trial.

If the effect of a decision of the Supreme Court in accordance with its ordinary functions under the Constitution is to remove someone from office, or remove property from that person, then such a removal could not constitute a breach of the rights under Article 5(1)(d) or "unjust deprivation of property" within the meaning of Article 5(1)(j) because the removal and deprivation would be in accordance with the law: *Vanuaroroa v Natapei* [2011] VUSC 92 at 18.

Other infringements

In *Monthouel v Republic of Vanuatu* [2019] VUCA 37 at [21]-[27] the Court of Appeal held that there was arguably an infringement of the right to protection of the law in circumstances where there was evidence that a Minister had failed to provide any response to letters that could be understood as invoking a statutory right of appeal.

In *Nari v Republic of Vanuatu* [2015] VUSC 132 at [61] the submission was made that a law may be so vague and uncertain that a person would find it difficult to determine what conduct was prohibited or permitted and that this would offend a person's fundamental right to "protection of law". The argument was not specifically addressed but the claim of a breach of that right was rejected.

Article 5(1)(h): freedom of assembly and association

The right of freedom of assembly and association in Article 5(1)(h) does not protect the use of a name, slogan or logo of a political party if that involves passing off at common law. The restriction is within the scope of the legitimate public interest in "public order" referred to in the opening words of Article 5(1): *Salwai v The Union of Moderate Patis Committee (Inc)* [2012] VUCA 19 at [47]-[48].

Article 5(1)(i): freedom of movement

The right to freedom of movement was not infringed by restrictions on the movement of a vessel owned by the appellant imposed by the Office of the Maritime Regulator in circumstances where the appellants could come and go wherever and whenever they chose: *Monthouel v Republic of Vanuatu* [2019] VUCA 37 at [16].

Article 5(1)(j): privacy and unjust deprivation of property

"property"

In *Terra Holdings Ltd v Sope* [2012] VUCA 16 at [49] the Court of Appeal referred to the definition of "property" in the Interpretation Act:

(a)   money, goods, chose in action and land; and

(b)   obligations, easements and every description of estate, interest and profit, present or future, arising out of or incident to property as defined in paragraph (a).

The court said that "This definition reflects the ordinary concept in law of property, and we consider the same broad meaning must be applied in the application of Article 5(1)(j)."

Article 5(1)(j) is not confined to property which is owned by the applicant. A right of "occupation and use of a property acquired lawfully" is also protected under the paragraph: *Vanuatu Copra and Cocoa Exporters Ltd v Republic of Vanuatu* [2006] VUSC 74 at 7.

In *Groupe Nairobi (Vanuatu) Ltd v Government of the Republic of Vanuatu* [2009] VUCA 35 at 13 the Court of Appeal held that there was no enforceable legal right to a tax refund. An expectation on the part of the appellant that it would receive a refund did not constitute property that could be the subject of unjust deprivation within the meaning of Article 5(1)(j).

What is the protection of "other property"?

The protection of "other property" in Article 5(1)(j) could be read as limited to the privacy of that property ("protection for the privacy of the home and other property") or more generally as protection of property ("protection for … property"). The language used in the paragraph is more consistent with the first interpretation but in *Ming v Republic of Vanuatu* [2021] VUSC 29 at [114] the emphasis given to the words suggests the second interpretation. The issue would only need to be resolved in a case where the protection of the "other property" was not from a breach of privacy or unjust deprivation.

"unjust deprivation of property"

In *Francois v Ozols* [1998] VUCA 5 the Court of Appeal said in relation to the protection against "unjust deprivation of property":

> The purpose of Article 5 is to protect the individual against arbitrary or unjust treatment by the organs of government through which the affairs of the Republic are administered. The protection of private rights between individuals, as opposed to the protection of rights between the individual and the Republic, is ensured by other provisions of the Constitution, namely the provisions of Chapter 4 that establish Parliament to make laws for the peace, order and good government of Vanuatu, the provisions of Chapter 7 that establish the Executive to implement those laws, and the provisions of Chapter 8 which establish the Judiciary to enable individuals to enforce them.

> For example, the protection afforded by Article 5(1)(f) [intended to be a reference to Article 5(1)(j)] against "unjust deprivation of property" is a protection against seizure or confiscation by government action. The general law already provides a comprehensive package of rules to protect against the invasion of commercial, economic or proprietary interests of one person by another person. Such rights are protected by the criminal law, and by civil laws such as the laws of contract and torts. In one sense if one person steals the goods of another, the victim of the theft has suffered an "unjust deprivation of property", but that injustice is not one that finds protection in Article 5. The injustice would be met by prosecution of the offender under the criminal law, and by civil action under the general law by the victim against the thief to recover the goods or their value.

What constitutes an "unjust" deprivation of property was considered in *Groupe Nairobi (Vanuatu) Ltd v Government of the Republic of Vanuatu* [2009] VUCA 35 at 14-16:

> Again, we consider the principles developed by the European Court under Article 1 of the First Protocol of the UCHR are instructive. Once a deprivation of property is found to have occurred it is necessary to examine whether the deprivation was lawful, whether it was in the public interest, and whether a reasonable and fair balance was struck between the public interest and individual rights… Whether the deprivation is lawful turns on whether it has occurred in accordance with the substantive and procedural requirements of the law…

In our opinion the notion of "unjust deprivation" in Article 5(j) is not confined solely to whether the deprivation occurred in accordance with law, and in that sense was not arbitrary. The notion also incorporates consideration of whether the act which effects the deprivation can be justified in the public interest having regard to the considerations discussed by the European Court.

In considering the public interest, the Supreme Court, as the body with responsibility for determining constitutional rights in Vanuatu, must allow Parliament a wide margin of appreciation in determining where the public interest lies. This will be particularly so where the legislative provisions concerned the allocation of public resources, as is the case with taxation and welfare laws. In considering whether a fair balance has been struck issues of compensation may in some cases be a relevant consideration. However this will depend on the kind of property right in question. If the right is one arising under the general law the question of compensation for the removal of that right may be an important consideration. However in the case of taxation and welfare laws the situation is different.

Although these statements were made in the context of a tax case, they have general application: *Stage Four Ltd v Proprietors of Strata Plan 0011* [2023] VUCA 36 at [38].

In *Stage Four Ltd v Proprietors of Strata Plan 0011* [2023] VUCA 36 at [31]-[33] the Court of Appeal noted that a change in the mechanics by which boundaries of lots and common property in a strata title scheme may be altered did not, of itself, effect any unjust deprivation of property. However it did not decide the case on that basis because it did not have the benefit of argument as to whether only a direct deprivation or deprivation by the government was necessary to invoke the constitutional protection.

If the effect of an order of a court is to remove property or money from a litigant, such removal could not constitute "unjust deprivation of property" within the meaning of Article 5(1)(f) as the deprivation would be one effected in accordance with the law: *Francois v Ozols* [1998] VUCA 5 at 12; see also *Vanuatu Copra and Cocoa Exporters Ltd v Republic of Vanuatu* [2006] VUSC 74 at 8-9; *Vanuaroroa v Natapei* [2011] VUSC 92 at 18.

Case examples

In *Kippion v Attorney-General* [1994] VUSC 1 an injunction was granted and orders were made for compensation of landowners whose food crops and timber had been damaged by the construction of a power line across their land without any lawful justification.

In *Panketo v Natuman* [2003] VUSC 117 a non-citizen whose property had been taken from him when he went into custody and was then stolen when it was in the custody of prison authorities obtained compensation because his Article 5(1)(j) right was likely to be infringed. He also obtained an order that he not be deported until that compensation was paid.

Article 5(1)(k): equal treatment

Article 5(1)(k) is not a general guarantee of equality. It does not apply to discrimination by private entities. It does not provide for equality between individuals or groups or an obligation to accord equal treatment to others. It is concerned with the application of the law: *Bohn v Republic of Vanuatu* [2013] VUSC 48 at 10.

In *Bohn v Republic of Vanuatu* [2013] VUSC 48 provisions of the Representation of the People Act [CAP 146] which required candidates for rural constituencies to be "a native or a person originating from that rural constituency" were held to be invalid because they discriminated on the grounds of "race" or "place of origin" and were not justified in accordance with the opening words of Article 5(1).

The imposition of obligations upon leaders under the Leadership Code Act [CAP 240] does not contravene Article 5(1)(k) because the Constitution itself identifies leaders as a separate and permissible category for which Parliament is mandated to specifically legislate: *Nari v Republic of Vanuatu* [2015] VUSC 132 at [33].

Article 5(2)(a): hearing within a reasonable time

The consideration of whether or not there has been unreasonable delay is not a mathematical calculation but must be determined on a consideration of the particular facts of each case: *Public Prosecutor v Emelee* [2005] VUCA 11 at 19.

In assessing whether there has been an infringement of the right to trial without unreasonable delay it is necessary to take into account the legitimate public interest in, among other things, public order as referred to in the chapeau to Article 5(1): *Public Prosecutor v Emelee* [2005] VUCA 11 at 10, 19.

A person should not be entitled to plead undue delay unless the person has taken such an earlier opportunity as there may have been to protest at the delay after that point: *Public Prosecutor v Emelee* [2005] VUCA 11 at 17.

In *Public Prosecutor v Silas* [2013] VUSC 48 an adjournment of a criminal case at the request of the prosecution was refused because the effect would be to deny the defendant a trial within a reasonable time. The Supreme Court said (at [8]):

> This constitutional provision is to be construed as requiring a satisfactory or reasonable explanation from the prosecution for delaying a trial reached in the usual course; as was the case here. The reasonableness of the time to try the case is not just a consideration of the actual months involved but all the surrounding circumstances including any prejudice to the defendant.

Article 5(2)(a): lawyer for a serious offence

In *Naling v Public Prosecutor* [1983] VULawRp 1; [1980-1994] Van LR 61 at 2 the Court of Appeal said that the provision "makes it clear that the time an accused is to be told of and afforded this fundamental right is either before the charge is read to him or immediately afterwards, before plea is taken".

The "afford" in the expression "be afforded a lawyer" means "give", "make available", "provide" or "supply": *Naling v Public Prosecutor* [1983] VULawRp 1; [1980-1994] Van LR 61 at 2.

In *Kalmet v Public Prosecutor* [1987] VULawRp 1; [1980-1994] Van LR 23 at 4 the Supreme Court explained the use of the word "serious" in "serious offence" is "a question of fact having regard to the whole matter in each case". In that case it held that the offence of "touching the body of a woman" contrary to s 98(2) of the Penal Code, constituted by grabbing a woman walking along a street on multiple occasions, was not a "serious offence" for the purposes of the constitutional provision. However this approach was disapproved in *Naling v Public Prosecutor* [1983] VULawRp 1; [1980-1994] Van LR 61 at 2 because of the practical difficulty in determining seriousness of the "whole matter" at the early stage at which it needs to be determined. The Court, in obiter dicta, said that the concept of "a serious offence" did not extend to any offence carrying any term of imprisonment. It decided that an offence carrying a maximum penalty of 10 years imprisonment was a serious offence and was not a "borderline case". It made reference (at 2-3) to the use that may be put of the threshold provided for the provision of legal aid in legal aid legislation.

In *Kilman v Attorney-General* [1997] VUSC 3 at 7-9 the Supreme Court held that:

(a)   Article 5(2)(a) is to be read with Article 56 which provides that the role of the Public Solicitor is to provide legal assistance to "needy persons".

(b)   Article 5(2)(a) does not provide an absolute right to an accused person to have the person's lawyer of choice but rather the person must rely upon the legal services that are offered by the State and that are readily available to the State, namely through the office of the Public Solicitor.

The statement in *Kilman* as to the relationship between Article 5(2)(a) and Article 56 was approved in *Office of the Public Solicitor v Kalsakau* [2005] VUCA 13 at 3.

In *Office of the Public Solicitor v Kalsakau* [2005] VUCA 13, a Member of Parliament, was found not to be entitled to assistance as he was not a "needy person".

The right in Article 5(2)(a) does not require that, in order for evidence of an interview with police to be admissible, an accused person must be informed, in a language the person understands, prior to the interview, of the person's right to legal counsel: *Leo v Public Prosecutor* [2008] VUCA 19.

Article 5(2)(b): presumption of innocence

In *Boedoro v Carcasses* [2015] VUCA 2 at [21], the power of the Parliament to suspend a Member of Parliament under Standing Order 40(4) for conduct outside Parliament was read subject to Article 5(2)(a) and (b), so that factual matters alleged against the Member were required to be proved in a court if they were to form the basis for suspension under that Standing Order.

Article 5(2)(h) double jeopardy

Proceedings under the Leadership Code Act [CAP 240] for the dismissal and disqualification of leaders who were convicted of bribery offences do not involve any infringement of the right in Article 5(2)(h) as the Leadership Code Act does not create offences and can never be the subject of a prosecution: *Tapangararua v Public Prosecutor* [2016] VUCA 10 at [44].

Corporations

While corporations are within the expression "all persons" in the opening words of Article 5(1) they do not enjoy all of the rights set out in Article 5(1): *Kilbride Ltd v Republic of Vanuatu* [2020] VUCA 24 at [6]-[11]. Companies do not have the rights set out in Article 5(1)(a), (b) and (c): *Stage Four Ltd v Proprietors of Strata Plan 0011* [2023] VUCA 36 at [12]. They do enjoy the rights set out in Article 5(1)(d), (j) and (k): *Vanuatu Copra and Cocoa Exporters Ltd v Republic of Vanuatu* [2006] VUSC 74 at 6-7; *Stage Four Ltd v Proprietors of Strata Plan 0011* [2023] VUCA 36 at [13].

The holding that corporations may have some of the rights in Article 5(1) means that in relation to those rights there is the potential for such corporations to be in a better position than "non-citizens and holders of dual citizenship who are not indigenous or naturalised citizens" (see commentary on Article 5: chapeau above) because Parliament has a general power to exclude the latter from the enjoyment of the rights in Article 5(1). In contrast, in relation to corporations there is no such general power to qualify their applicable Article 5(1) rights and it is necessary that any qualification fit within the concept of "respect for the rights and freedoms of others and … the legitimate public interest in defence, safety, public order, welfare and health". Given the potential breadth of those concepts, the difference in position between corporations and non-citizens may not be of great practical significance.

Effect of Article 7

Although the obligations in Article 7 are not justiciable, Article 7(f) has been taken into account in determining whether an entitlement under Article 5 has been infringed: *Stage Four Ltd v Proprietors of Strata Plan 0011* [2023] VUCA 36 at [45].

Judicial errors

In *Mass v Government of the Republic of Vanuatu* [2018] VUCA 11 at [61]-[62] the Court of Appeal identified that no breach of a fundamental right occurs where an error of law or procedure has been made but is corrected according to law.

Relationship with Article 77 and 80

In *Kilbride Ltd v Republic of Vanuatu* [2020] VUCA 24 at [38] the Court of Appeal said that "Articles at 77 [Compensation] and 80 [Government may own land] do not create a power that authorises Parliament to legislate in any way that lessens the scope and operation of Article 5".

Case examples

Siri v Government of the Republic of Vanuatu [2024] VUSC 196 – police entry into house to recover government property.

Quinto v Republic of Vanuatu [2020] VUSC 53 – no constitutional cause of action arising under Article 5(1)(c) and (d) arising from the issue of a residence permit to a person who subsequently assaulted the applicants – "There may be appropriate cases or circumstances where the failure of government or its instrumentalities in breach of their statutory functions may amount to breach of fundamental rights. But the circumstances of the present case were not such cases or circumstances" (at [47]).

Hilltop Ltd v Minister of Lands [2019] VUSC 121 – the acquisition of an easement (where there were cables and pipelines transporting electricity, fuel, gas, water and communication lines) claimed to be in breach of the owner's rights under Article 5(1)(j) and (k) was found to be within the scope of the qualification "the legitimate public interest in defence, safety, public order, welfare and health".

Mass v Government of the Republic of Vanuatu [2018] VUCA 11 at [63] – the Court of Appeal, when assessing a claim of breach of Article 5 as a result of delay in court proceedings, referred to the qualification on Article 5 and said: "The limited resources of the court must in the public interest and for good public order be fairly shared between all those who come to court."

Makenock v Republic of Vanuatu [2006] VUSC 104 – the applicant had been unlawfully detained by police over several months and was found to be entitled to compensation – s 40 of the Police Act [CAP 105] which provided that there was no liability for acts done in good faith had no application in the case of breaches of rights enshrined in guarantees under the Constitution.

Working Group for Justice v Government of the Republic of Vanuatu [2002] VUSC 55 – Supreme Court awarded compensation to be assessed to 33 plaintiffs who had been arrested and significantly ill-treated by police – rights in Article 5 (1) (a), (b), (c), (d), (e), (i), (j) and (k) found to have been breached.

6. Enforcement of fundamental rights

(1)   Anyone who considers that any of the rights guaranteed to him by the Constitution has been, is being or is likely to be infringed may, independently of any other possible legal remedy, apply to the Supreme Court to enforce that right.

(2)   The Supreme Court may make such orders, issue such writs and give such directions, including the payment of compensation, as it considers appropriate to enforce the right.

Constitutional Committee

A provision for enforcement of the rights by the Supreme Court was included in the first working paper on fundamental rights.[34] It was described by Professor Zorgbibe as "inspired by a British-style system with a Supreme Court able to give injunctions etc to protect those rights".[35] Its terms were refined in a subsequent working paper[36] and the Article was approved along with the balance of the Chapter on 17 September 1979.[37]

Commentary

Article 6(1)

In *In the matter of the infant P* [1984] VULawRp 1; [1980-1994] Van LR 130 at 3 the Court of Appeal described Article 6(1) as "extremely wide" and said that it was open to proceed by an application under that provision even if the claimant could have proceeded by way of an appeal.

The existence of an entitlement to seek judicial review does not prevent reliance upon Article 5 rights in proceedings brought under Article 6: *Emelee v Republic of Vanuatu* [2024] VUSC 193 at [19]; *Willie v Public Service Commission* [1993] VULawRp 5; [1980-1994] Van LR 634 at 4.

Article 6(2)

In *Republic of Vanuatu v Benard* [2016] VUCA 4 at [20] the Court of Appeal pointed out that a monetary award for an infringement of a fundamental right or freedom is an award made under public law compensation principles, not common law damages and the focus of the claim must be on the breach of rights, not personal injury. At [28] the Court addressed the possibility of a claimant pursuing both common law and constitutional remedies, saying:

> In an appropriate case it could be open to a person to pursue both avenues of remedy, but double compensation will not be allowed.

At [34]-[36] the Court addressed the nature of compensation available under Article 6:

> 34. In assessing compensation to be paid for an established breach of a constitutional right consideration of the nature of the wrongdoing that attracts the right to compensation must be of central importance. The more serious the malice or knowing conduct that renders the breach sufficiently serious to warrant compensation, the greater will be the need to make an award that adequately demonstrates that seriousness and will demonstrate the need for respect of the fundamental rights or rights that have been infringed.

---

[34] Working paper G2: FCO107/107.

[35] Minutes 27; PV6[8].

[36] Working paper G6, Article 3: Minutes 240; FCO 107/108.

[37] Minutes 175 (PV50[42]).

35. As a starting point compensation should make a good actual pecuniary losses suffered by the victim, like special damages in a common-law action make good out-of-pocket expenses. If personal injury or damage to business or reputation of the kind which attracts general damages in a common-law assessment is suffered compensation for that should be recognised, and again common-law principles may provide by analogy a useful guide.

36. But beyond compensation for those items, common-law principles as to punitive damages are likely to be of little assistance. Depending on the flagrantcy of the conduct constituting the breach of the constitutional rights the compensatory award may be lower than would be an award at common law, or might be much higher.

See also *Emelee v Republic of Vanuatu* [2024] VUSC 193 at [22].

Procedural requirements

Applications to the Supreme Court under Article 6 are subject to the Constitutional Procedures Rules 2003. Rule 2.2 requires a proceeding under Article 6 or Article 53(1) to be commenced by filing a Constitutional Application in the Supreme Court. Rule 2.4 requires that the Republic of Vanuatu be the respondent to the application. Constitutional questions arising in other proceedings will not be determined: *Rombu v Family Rasu* [2006] VUCA 22 at 4.

In *Mass v Government of the Republic of Vanuatu* [2018] VUCA 11 at [32], the Court of Appeal said that "Articles 6 and 53 do not provide that after an application is made the claim for redress can proceed regardless of well-recognised procedural and substantive law principles that control the ordinary trial of disputed questions of fact and law."

Prior to the making of the Constitutional Procedures Rules in 2003, constitutional applications were governed by s 218 of the Criminal Procedure Code [CAP 136]: see *Republic of Vanuatu v Picchi* [2001] VUCA 6 at 4.

Limitation Act does not apply

The terms of Article 6 and the terms of the Limitation Act [CAP 212] mean that the Limitation Act does not apply to an application made under Article 6: *Tangraro v Republic of Vanuatu* [2018] VUSC 198 at [24]-[30].

However, where there is substantial delay in bringing a claim, the delay may be taken into account in determining whether interest is payable on any compensation: for example, *Wokon v Government of the Republic of Vanuatu* [2006] VUSC 25 at 6, 14.

Henderson v Henderson estoppel

The principle in *Henderson v Henderson* (1843) 67 ER 319 applies to proceedings under Article 6 so that it is not open, in fresh proceedings, to make a claim which should have been brought in earlier proceedings between the same parties: *Amos v Republic of Vanuatu* [2017] VUSC 72 at [10]-[11]. It could be expected that the same approach would be taken to proceedings under Article 53.

Application of Article 6 to the Supreme Court

In *Picchi v Attorney-General* [2001] VUSC 106 at 3 the Supreme Court held that Article 6 involved in exercise of original jurisdiction and that there was an obligation to enquire into the conduct of another judge, even a fellow judge of equal rank.

In *Kalnpel v Government of the Republic of Vanuatu* [2023] VUCA 10 at [29]-[30] the Court of Appeal expressed the tentative view that applications under Article 6 are not available in respect of decisions of the Supreme Court. The Court did not refer to the earlier decision in *Picchi*.

Res judicata/issue estoppel

In *Picchi v Attorney-General* [2001] VUSC 106 at 4 the Supreme Court held that in proceedings under Article 6 and 53 it was not bound by findings of fact made in an earlier criminal appeal as the remedies in those articles are provided "independently of" or "without prejudice to" any other legal remedy.

Difference between Article 6 and Article 53

Article 6 is wider in scope than Article 53 because it may apply where the Constitution "has been, is being *or is likely to be* infringed" whereas article 53 only applies where a provision of the Constitution "has been infringed": *Kilman v Natapei* [2011] VUCA 24 at [13]; *Toama v Republic of Vanuatu* [2016] VUSC 1 at [3].

Part II – Fundamental Duties

7. Fundamental duties

Every person has the following fundamental duties to himself and his descendants and to others –

    (a)   to respect and to act in the spirit of the Constitution;

    (b)   to recognise that he can fully develop his abilities and advance his true interests only by active participation in the development of the national community;

    (c)   to exercise the rights guaranteed or conferred by the Constitution and to use the opportunities made available to him under it to participate fully in the government of the Republic of Vanuatu;

    (d)   to protect the Republic of Vanuatu and to safeguard the national wealth, resources and environment in the interests of the present generation and of future generations;

<table>
<tr><td>(e)</td><td>to work according to his talents in socially useful employment and, if necessary, to create for himself legitimate opportunities for such employment;</td></tr>
<tr><td>(f)</td><td>to respect the rights and freedoms of others and to cooperate fully with others in the interests of interdependence and solidarity;</td></tr>
<tr><td>(g)</td><td>to contribute, as required by law, according to his means, to the revenues required for the advancement of the Republic of Vanuatu and the attainment of national objectives;</td></tr>
<tr><td>(h)</td><td>in the case of a parent, to support, assist and educate all his children, legitimate and illegitimate, and in particular to give them a true understanding of their fundamental rights and duties and of the national objectives and of the culture and customs of the people of Vanuatu;</td></tr>
<tr><td>(i)</td><td>in the case of a child, to respect his parents.</td></tr>
</table>

Constitutional Committee

Only fundamental rights were included in early working papers on this topic.[38] The fundamental duties were included as a result of a proposal by Tabwemassana[39] and brought together with fundamental rights and enforcement in a subsequent working paper.[40]

The words "legitimate and illegitimate" were inserted in the draft of Article 7(h) on 17 September 1979.[41]

---

8. Fundamental duties non-justiciable but public authorities to encourage compliance

Except as provided by law, the fundamental duties are non-justiciable. Nevertheless it is the duty of all public authorities to encourage compliance with them so far as lies within their respective powers.

Constitutional Committee

This provision was not in the originally proposed draft[42] but was added as part of the legislative drafting process and approved at the last meeting of the Committee on 17 September 1979.[43]

---

[38] Working papers G2 (FCO107/107) and G3 (Minutes 237 (French)).
[39] Working papers G4 (Minutes 239) and G5 (Minutes 238).
[40] Working paper G6: Minutes 240-241; FCO107/108.
[41] Minutes 175 (PV50[40]).
[42] Working paper G6: Minutes at 240; FCO 107/108.
[43] Minutes 175 (PV50[41]).

Commentary

While the fundamental duties in Article 7 are not justiciable against individuals, the duties of the authorities and government under Article 8 are enforceable under Article 53: *Timikata v Attorney-General* [1992] VULawRp 9; [1980-1994] Van LR 575; *Kilbride Ltd v Republic of Vanuatu* [2020] VUCA 24 at [13].

CHAPTER 3 – CITIZENSHIP

Constitutional Committee

The issue of citizenship received considerable attention from the Committee. The principal discussion was on 30 July, 7 and 8 August 1979[44] and Chapter 3 was then approved without further discussion on 17 September 1979.[45] The issues of automatic citizenship, the preconditions to naturalisation and dual citizenship were the principal issues discussed and the outcome of those discussions is reflected in the original provisions of the Constitution.

The issue of citizenship was a significant one so far as the British Government was concerned. The British Resident Commissioner submitted to the Committee that persons born in the country should be given the country's citizenship.[46] However, after the Committee had approved the citizenship provisions the Commissioner made it clear that the British Government accepted them in order to "promote agreement and help the New Hebrides move towards a constitution approved by all".[47]

9. Automatic citizens

On the Day of Independence the following persons shall automatically become citizens of Vanuatu –

(a) a person who has or had four grandparents who belong to a tribe or community indigenous to Vanuatu; and

(b) a person of ni-Vanuatu ancestry who has no citizenship, nationality or the status of an optant.

Constitutional Committee

This article was approved by the Committee on 8 August 1979.[48]

Commentary

Although not made clear by the minutes of the Committee, the reference in Article 9(b) to a person with "the status of an optant" would have been understood as a person, other than a citizen of Britain or France, who had opted under Article 1(2) of the Anglo French Protocol of 1914[49] to be governed by the

---

44 Minutes 71 (PV25[2]); 94-96 (PV31[1]-[20]); 97-98 (PV32[1]-[16]).
45 Minutes 175 (PV50[43]).
46 Minutes 90; see also Minutes 71 (PV 25[2]).
47 Minutes 119 (PV38[6]).
48 Minutes 97 (PV32[4]). An earlier draft was approved the day before: Minutes 95 (PV31[6]).
49 UK Treaty Series No 7 (1922).

legal system applicable to the subjects or citizens of one or other of the Britain or France. Article 1(2) of the Protocol provided:

> 2. The subjects or citizens of other Powers shall enjoy the same rights and shall be subject to the same obligations as British subjects or French citizens. They must opt within one month, by means of a declaration made either verbally or by letter to the Resident Commissioner concerned or his delegate, for the legal system applicable to the subjects or citizens of one or other of the two Powers. Such option shall, moreover, be compulsory even before the expiration of the above period, if the person concerned has committed any action involving the application of the laws of one or other of the two Powers or of the joint regulations in force in the Group. Failing such option, or in the case of death before option, the Resident Commissioners acting jointly shall decide under which system the persons concerned shall be placed. Foreign labourers introduced into the Group by or with the authority of one or other of the two Governments shall be regarded during the whole period of their residence in the Group as dependents of the Power whose Government is concerned.

---

10. Entitlement to citizenship

Every person who on the Day of Independence is a person of ni-Vanuatu ancestry and has the nationality or citizenship of a foreign state or the status of an optant shall become a citizen of Vanuatu if he makes an application, or an application is made on his behalf by his parent or lawful guardian.

Constitutional Committee

The original Article was discussed and approved at the meeting on 8 August 1979.[50] The final form of chapter 3 was approved by the Committee on 17 September 1979.[51]

Amendments

The original Article 10 provided:

> 10. Every person who on the day of Independence is a person of New Hebridean ancestry and has the nationality or citizenship of a foreign state or the status of an optant shall become a citizen of the New Hebrides if he makes an application, or an application is made on his behalf by his parent or lawful guardian, within 3 months of the day of Independence or such longer period as Parliament may prescribe. The New Hebrides citizenship of such a person shall automatically lapse if he has not renounced his other citizenship or nationality within 3 months of the granting of New Hebridean citizenship or such longer period as Parliament may prescribe, except that in the case of a person under the age of 18 years the period of renunciation shall be 3 months after he has reached the age of 18 years.

As a result of the Constitution (Sixth) (Amendment) Act No 27 of 2013 the words in Article 10 were amended by the deletion of the words appearing after

---

[50] Minutes 97-98 (PV32[3]-[16]).
[51] Minutes 175 (PV50[43]).

"lawful guardian". That had the effect of removing the requirement for renunciation of citizenship or nationality of another country. Recognition of dual citizenship, as reflected in the amended Article 13, was inserted at the same time.

Commentary

As to the meaning of "optant" see the commentary on Article 9 above.

---

11. Persons born after day of independence

Anyone born after the Day of Independence, whether in Vanuatu or abroad, shall become a citizen of Vanuatu if at least one of his parents is a citizen of Vanuatu.

---

12. Naturalisation

A national of a foreign state or a stateless person may apply to be naturalised as a citizen of Vanuatu if he has lived continuously in Vanuatu for at least 10 years immediately before the date of the application.

Parliament may prescribe further conditions of the eligibility to apply for naturalisation and shall provide for the machinery to review and decide on applications for naturalisation.

Constitutional Committee

The period of residence before an application for naturalisation was discussed at the meetings of the Committee on 7 and 8 August 1979.[52] Six years and 18 years were proposed. On 8 August 1979 the period of 10 years was fixed upon.[53]

---

13. Recognition of dual citizenship

(1) The Republic of Vanuatu recognises dual citizenship.

(2) A person who is a citizen of Vanuatu or of a state other than Vanuatu may be granted dual citizenship.

(3) For the purposes of protecting the national sovereignty of Vanuatu, a holder of dual citizenship must not:

    (a)   hold or serve in any public office; and

    (b)   be involved in Vanuatu politics; and

    (c)   fund activities that would cause political instability in Vanuatu; and

---

[52]   Minutes 95 (PV31[7]-[13]); 98 (PV32[16]).
[53]   Minutes 98 (PV32[16]).

(d)   affiliate with or form any political parties in Vanuatu;

(e)   stand as a candidate and vote at any of the following elections:

    (i)   general election for Members to Parliament; and

    (ii) provincial election for members to a Provincial Government Council; and

    (iii) municipal election for members to a Municipal Council.

(4)   To avoid doubt, subarticle (3) does not apply to an indigenous citizen or a person who has gained Vanuatu citizenship by naturalisation, who hold dual citizenship.

(5)   Parliament may prescribe:

(a)   the requirements to be met by categories of persons applying for dual citizenship; or

(b)   the privileges to be accorded to any category of persons who are holders of dual citizenship.

Constitutional Committee

As originally drafted, Article 13 provided that the Republic did not recognise dual nationality. The draft Article which became Article 13 was approved by the Committee on 7 August 1979.[54]

Amendments

The original terms of Article 13 were:

> 13. The Republic of the New Hebrides does not recognise dual nationality. Any citizen of the New Hebrides who is or becomes a citizen of another state shall cease to be a citizen of the New Hebrides unless he renounces that other citizenship within 3 months of acquiring New Hebridean citizenship or that other citizenship, as the case may be, or such longer period as Parliament may prescribe, except that in the case of a person under the age of 18 years the period of renunciation shall be 3 months after he has reached the age of 18 years.

The Article was repealed and substituted by the Constitution (Sixth) (Amendment) Act No 27 of 2013 which inserted Article 13 in its current form.

Commentary

Article 13(3)(a): public office

The expression "public office" is used in Articles 13(3)(a), 57(2) and 90(3). The expression is not defined in the Constitution. An Act which expressly states that an office is not a "public office" where, for constitutional purposes, the nature of that office would lead it to be characterised as a "public office" is inconsistent

---

with the Constitution and would be invalid: *President of the Republic of Vanuatu v Speaker of the Parliament* [2023] VUSC 33 at [41]-[43]. In that case the position of a "Special Envoy" which involved "representing the Republic of Vanuatu on a specific matter in dealings with another State" was found to be a "public office" for the purposes of the Constitution.

---

14. Further provision for citizenship

Parliament may make provision for the acquisition of citizenship of Vanuatu by persons not covered in the preceding Articles of this Chapter and may make provision for the deprivation and renunciation of citizenship of Vanuatu.

Constitutional Committee

The original proposal in a working paper of the Committee[55] allowed the Parliament to bestow citizenship on a person who was not, or was no longer, capable of acquiring citizenship pursuant to the other provisions of the Constitution. On 7 August 1979 Professor Ghai suggested that this be replaced with a general statement allowing Parliament to make further provision concerning the acquisition, deprivation and renunciation of citizenship and that proposal was approved.[56]

---

55   Working paper H1: FCO107/107.
56   Minutes 96 (PV31[17]).

CHAPTER 4 – PARLIAMENT

Commentary

The powers and privileges of Parliament are not specified in the Constitution. When the privileges of Parliament are defined by law they will be subject to the Constitution and the guarantees of fundamental rights enshrined in the Constitution: *Korman v Parliament of the Republic of Vanuatu* [2011] VUSC 304 at 11.

The powers of Parliament do not extend to finding a member in "contempt of the Constitution as the Constitution places the duty and responsibility of all constitutional questions or challenges in the Supreme Court": *Korman v Parliament of the Republic of Vanuatu* [2011] VUSC 304 at 7-8.

15. Parliament

The legislature shall consist of a single chamber which shall be known as Parliament.

Constitutional Committee

The first working paper on the Parliament that was considered by the Committee[57] included two houses: the "National Assembly" and the "Senate or Council of Chiefs". The Senate or Council of Chiefs was not proposed to have legislative power, but was proposed to be a body required to be consulted on matters of tradition and custom and available to be consulted on ordinary legislation.

16. Power to make laws

(1)   Parliament may make laws for the peace, order and good government of Vanuatu.

(2)   Parliament shall make laws by passing bills introduced either by one or more members or by the Prime Minister or a Minister.

(3)   When a bill has been passed by Parliament it shall be presented to the President of the Republic who shall assent to it within 2 weeks.

(4)   If the President considers that the bill is inconsistent with a provision of the Constitution he shall refer it to the Supreme Court for its opinion. The bill shall not be promulgated if the Supreme Court considers it inconsistent with a provision of the Constitution.

---

[57]   Working paper D1: FCO107/107.

Constitutional Committee

The text which became Article 16(1)-(2) was only subject to limited discussion and was approved at the meeting on 1 August 1979.[58]

On 17 September 1979 the Committee considered a clause that required the President to assent to a bill "forthwith". Concern was expressed that an obstructive President could refuse to sign a bill. This led to approval of an amended draft which provided: "When a bill has been passed by Parliament, it shall be presented to the President of the Republic, who shall assent to it forthwith. In case the President has not signed the bill within two weeks of its presentation to him, the bill shall become law".[59]

At the Constitutional Conference on 18 September 1979 a further draft,[60] which added what has become Article 16(4), was proposed by the French and British Ministers.[61] This allowed referral of a bill which the President considered to be inconsistent with a provision of the Constitution to the Supreme Court. This change was adopted and was reflected in the final form of the Article.

Commentary

Article 16(1)

The use of the language "peace, order and good government" is designed to achieve, subject to the terms of the Constitution, a plenary legislative power: *Virelala v Ombudsman* [1997] VUSC 35 at 24; *President v Speaker* [2009] VUSC 25 at 6. The courts do not engage in any enquiry as to whether the proposed Act is, in fact, "for the peace, order and good government of Vanuatu": *Timakata v Attorney-General* [1992] VULawRp 9; [1980-1994] Van LR 575 at 15. Nor do the courts conduct any enquiry into the motives of the Parliament: *President of the Republic of Vanuatu v Attorney-General* [1998] VUSC 18.

There is no constitutional obligation upon the Parliament to consult prior to making laws: *President v Speaker* [2009] VUSC 25 at 5; *Government of the Republic of Vanuatu v President of the Republic of Vanuatu* [2012] VUSC 109 at 20.

A contract entered into by the Republic cannot exclude or effectively fetter the authority of Parliament to legislate, or fetter the lawful exercise by the executive government of delegated powers provided under legislation: *Northern Island Stevedoring Company Ltd v Republic of Vanuatu* [2025] VUCA 26 at [17]-[18].

---

[58]   Minutes 81 (PV27[18]). The text of Article 5 in working paper D1 is at Minutes 232 and reflected in Article 5 in working paper D1(7) presented to the Committee on 5 September 1979: Minutes 130 (PV41[2]).

[59]   Minutes 175-176 (PV50[44]-[46]).

[60]   Working paper D1(11): FCO107/109.

[61]   Minutes 177 (PV 51[2]).

Article 16(2)

This provision makes it clear that bills may be introduced by one or more members of the Parliament, the Prime Minister or a Minister. Article 25(3) provides a limitation on motions that would levy or increase taxation or require expenditure of public funds if the motion is not supported by the Government.

Article 16(3)

A bill will only become an Act of the Parliament after it has received assent from the President: *Acts of Parliament Act* [CAP 116] s 5(2). The President is obliged to grant assent to the bill under Article 16(3) unless the President considers it to be unconstitutional in which case the bill must be referred to the Supreme Court for its opinion under Article 16(4): *Government of the Republic of Vanuatu v President of the Republic of Vanuatu* [2012] VUSC 109 at 18-19.

If the President fails to assent to a bill that has been passed by Parliament within two weeks or refer it to the Supreme Court under Article 16(4) this constitutes an infringement of Article 16 and remedies may be obtained under Article 53: *Government of the Republic of Vanuatu v President of the Republic of Vanuatu* [2012] VUSC 109 at 20-21.

Article 16(4)

The operation of Article 16(4) occurs after the passing of the Bill by Parliament and before its promulgation. It is therefore "within and during the law making process" which is different from other Commonwealth jurisdictions: *President of the Republic of Vanuatu v Speaker of Parliament* [2000] VUSC 43.

In *Attorney-General v Timakata* [1993] VUCA 2 at 5 the Court of Appeal addressed the operation of the reading down provisions of the Interpretation Act [CAP 132] in a referral under Article 16(4):

> There is no doubt that if the Bills had received the President's assent and had become law the ouster provisions would, if possible have been construed so that they did not conflict with article 5(1)(d). That however does not mean that they were not inconsistent with the Constitution within article 16(4). It was precisely because they would have been inconsistent with the Constitution, if passed into law that they would have been read down as a matter of construction if that could possibly have been done. It is not necessary to decide whether it would have been possible to interpret the ouster provisions in such a way that they would have been entirely consistent with the Constitution. One purpose of article 16(4) is to prevent laws which on their face appear to be inconsistent with the Constitution from being enacted. If the Bill is inconsistent with the Constitution it is not to be promulgated, and the citizen is thereby saved the trouble of deciding whether the offending provision can be read down so as not to apply to the circumstances of the particular case and spared the expense of having the question tested in the Courts.

> It may well be that for some purposes the provisions of the Interpretation Act can be regarded in deciding whether a Bill is unconstitutional. For instance if a Bill appeared to discriminate on the ground of sex because it used only masculine

expressions, regard could be had to the fact that if it became law words importing the masculine would include the feminine: See Interpretation Act section 3(2). However section 9 is in this respect exceptional; it applies only where there is a conflict between an Act and the Constitution. However where there appears to be a conflict between the Bill and the Constitution the President must refer the Bill to the Supreme Court and the Bill should not be promulgated if the Supreme Court holds that the inconsistency exists.

In *Saemon v Tallis* [2019] VUCA 44 at [23]-[25] the Court of Appeal said:

> Before turning to the contentions on this appeal, it is also important to note that the President's role under Article 16(4) of the Constitution is an important one. It is not a political one. Nor is it a discretionary decision. Once the President has formed an adverse view about a relevant Bill not complying with the Constitution, it is his duty to refer it to the Supreme Court for opinion.
>
> The President, as was said in President of the *Republic of Vanuatu v Speaker of Parliament* [2000] VUSC 43, Civil Case 051 of 2000 (11 August 2000), represents the constitutional check and balancing element between the function of the Executive Government and the function of the Legislative Government on the law making process.
>
> We adopt what the Chief Justice said concerning referral also to the decision in *Timakata v. Attorney-General* [1992] VU Law Rep 9; [1980-1994] Van LR 575 (1 November 1992).

A proposed law is presumed to be constitutional. The burden of persuading the Supreme Court that the proposed law is unconstitutional is on the referral authority under Article 16(4): *President of the Republic of Vanuatu v Speaker of Parliament* [2008] VUSC 77 at 6. In the same case the Court identified who should be the parties joined to any referral proceedings. This issue is now addressed by r 3.4 of the Constitutional Procedures Rules.

How the costs of a referral under Article 16(4) are paid was addressed in *President of the Republic of Vanuatu v Speaker of Parliament* [2000] VUSC 43.

When the President makes a referral under Article 16(4) it is appropriate to refer to the President as the "Referral Authority" and not the "Petitioner": *President of the Republic of Vanuatu v Speaker of Parliament* [2000] VUSC 43.

The Preamble to the Constitution is not a "provision of the Constitution" within the meaning of Article 16(4) of the Constitution: *President of the Republic of Vanuatu v Speaker of Parliament* [2008] VUSC 77 at 18, 28.

Partial invalidity on an Article 16(4) referral

In *President of the Republic of Vanuatu v Speaker of Parliament* [2000] VUSC 43 the Supreme Court said in relation to the potential for severance of an invalid provision:

> The situation which is of concern here is that of partial constitutionality of a bill or that of partial validation of a bill of Parliament. Is a bill valid in part, and invalid in part? In my view, if the valid part can stand by itself it will be sustained. This

means that the same bill may be in part constitutional and in part unconstitutional, and if the parts are wholly independent of each other, that which is constitutional may stand while that which is unconstitutional will be rejected. It must be noted that the parts of a bill must be separate and independent of each other if the valid portions are to be upheld.

In the earlier case of *Attorney-General v Timakata* [1993] VUCA 2 at 8 the Court of Appeal, having found two provisions wholly or partly inconsistent with the Constitution, decided that it was open for the Court to advise the President to assent to the remainder of the bill after excising the offending words because that was the approach agreed to by both parties in the Supreme Court and they were held to that position.

Referrals made

Referrals have been made in the following cases:

(a)   *Attorney-General v Timakata* [1993] VUCA 2 (re Broadcasting and Television Act No 3 of 1992 and Business License (Amendment) Act No 4 of 1992);

(b)   *President of the Republic of Vanuatu v Attorney-General* [1998] VUSC 18 (re Ombudsman (Repeal) Act No 15 of 1997);

(c)   *President of the Republic of Vanuatu v Speaker of Parliament* [2000] VUSC 43 (re Public Service (Amendment) Act No 18 of 2000 and Government (Amendment) Act No 23 of 2000);

(d)   *President of the Republic of Vanuatu v Speaker of Parliament* [2008] VUSC 77 (re Family Protection Act 2008);

(e)   *President of the Republic of Vanuatu v Speaker of Parliament* [2012] VUSC 183 (re Public Service (Amendment) Act No 1 of 2011);

(f)   *Saemon v Tallis* [2019] VUCA 44 (re Constitution (Seventh) (Amendment) Act No 1 of 2019);

(g)   *President of the Republic of Vanuatu v Speaker of the Parliament* [2023] VUSC 33 (re Foreign Services (Amendment) Act No 19 of 2021);

(h)   *President of the Republic of Vanuatu v Speaker of Parliament* [2025] VUSC 286 (re Constitution (Ninth) (Amendment) Act No 7 of 2025).

---

17. Election of members of Parliament

(1)   Parliament shall consist of members elected on the basis of universal franchise through an electoral system which includes an element of proportional representation so as to ensure fair representation of different political groups and opinions.

(2)   Subject to such conditions or restrictions as may be prescribed by Parliament every citizen of Vanuatu who is at least 25 years of age shall be eligible to stand for election to Parliament.

Constitutional Committee

The provision which became Article 17 was approved by the Committee on 6 August 1979.[62] It replaced more complicated and prescriptive language that had been proposed earlier in order to resolve divisions, reflected in the discussion on 2 August 1979, between those Committee members that favoured single member electorates and those who favoured a system involving proportional representation.[63] The approval by the Committee included two additional matters relating to the establishment of a committee to examine the electoral system. These were reflected in Article 9 of a further working paper[64] and incorporated into the Constitution as Article 93 (originally Article 91) in the Transitional Provisions chapter.

Commentary

Article 17(1)

Article 17(1) says that Parliament shall only consist of members who have been elected in a particular way: "It does not, in other words, define Parliament but limits the form and method of selection of its members": *Sope v Attorney-General (No 2)* [1988] VULawRp 13; [1980-1994] Van LR 363 at 10.

This provision provides guidance to the Parliament as to the electoral system but does not define with precision the requirements of the electoral system. The normative standards which must be met by the electoral system include the following:

(a)   members must be elected;

(b)   there must be a universal franchise;

(c)   there must be "an element of proportional representation so as to ensure fair representation of different political groups and opinions".

In *Kalpokas v Government of the Republic of Vanuatu* [1994] VUSC 9 at 3, the Supreme Court said, in relation to Article 17(1):

> What the Constitution does not require is that Parliament shall be elected by means of "suffrage universal direct" or "direct universal suffrage". Therefore there would be nothing unconstitutional were Parliament to be elected through the means of an electoral college. Whichever mode is preferred, direct or indirect, neither is unconstitutional.

Section 2(d) of the Members of Parliament (Vacation of Seats) Act [CAP 174], which vacates the seat of a Member who does not attend three consecutive sittings of the Parliament, is valid. In *Carlot v Attorney-General* [1988] VULawRp 21; [1980-1994] Van LR 407 at 2 the Court of Appeal said:

> The Constitution intends that the Republic shall be governed by Parliament. Parliament can only function if members attend. There is nothing

---

62   Minutes 91 (PV30[7]-[10]).

63   Minutes 83-85 (PV28[5]-[23]); 215 (working paper D1(4): Minutes 215).

64   D1(7): Minutes 232 (French); FCO 107/108.

unconstitutional in a provision designed to ensure that parliament does function, and that a person elected to parliament does what he is elected to do attend Parliament. If he fails to do so, it is reasonable that he should be replaced by somebody who will.

Section 17(2)

Article 17(2) defines the entitlement to stand for election to Parliament. It is necessary to be (a) a citizen of Vanuatu; (b) at least 25 years of age.

The "conditions or restrictions as may be prescribed by Parliament" are provided by the Representation of the People Act [CAP 146]: *Toama v Republic of Vanuatu* [2016] VUSC 1 at [10].

17A Vacation of seat where a member of Parliament resigns or is terminated for ceasing to support a political party

(1)　This Article applies to a member of Parliament if the member, having been a candidate of a political party and elected to parliament:

    (a)　　resigns from the political party; or

    (b)　　is terminated as a member of the political party for ceasing to support the political party.

(2)　The President of a political party must notify the Speaker in writing within 14 days after a member has resigned from, or has been terminated for ceasing to support, the political party in accordance with that political party's Constitution.

(3)　The Speaker must, within 7 days of receiving the notice under sub article (2), declare the seat of that member of Parliament vacant by Order published in the Gazette.

(4)　For the purposes of this Article, a member of Parliament representing a political party is deemed to have ceased support of the political party when he or she satisfies the grounds provided under the political party's Constitution that indicate when a member is deemed to have ceased support for the political party.

(5)　This Article applies despite the provisions of subarticle 5(1) of this Constitution.

Amendment

See annotations to Article 17B below.

17B Vacation of seat of an independent member

(1)   This Article applies to a member of Parliament who:

    (a)   is elected to Parliament as an independent candidate; or

    (b)   is the only member representing a political party; or

    (c)   is elected to Parliament representing a custom movement.

(2)   Within 3 months after the first day of the first sitting of Parliament at which the Speaker and the Prime Minister are elected, a member of Parliament referred to under sub article (1) must submit to the Clerk of Parliament a declaration of his or her affiliation to a political party represented in Parliament, in the form approved by the Clerk of Parliament and counter-signed by the political party's President.

(3)   In the case of a bi-election, a newly elected member of Parliament referred to under sub article (1) must, within 3 months after the first day of the next sitting of Parliament after that a bi-election, submit to the Clerk of Parliament a declaration of his or her affiliation to a political party represented in Parliament, in the form approved by the Clerk of Parliament and counter-signed by the political party's President.

(4)   At the next sitting of the Parliament:

    (a)   in the case of a general election-the Speaker must, having received affiliations under sub article (2), officially announce the affiliations of all members of Parliament; or

    (b)   in the case of a bi-election-the Speaker must, having received the newly elected member of Parliament's affiliation under subarticle (3), officially announce the affiliation of that member of Parliament.

(5)   A member of Parliament who fails to make a declaration under subarticle (2) or (3) is deemed to have vacated his or her seat at the end of the 3 month period referred to in that subarticle.

(6)   The President of a political party must notify the Speaker in writing within 14 days after a member of Parliament has ceased to be affiliated with the political party in accordance with the political party's Constitution.

(7)   The Speaker must, within 7 days of receiving the notice under subarticle (6), declare the seat of the member of Parliament vacant by Order published in the Gazette.

(8)   For the purposes of this Article, a member of Parliament is deemed to have ceased to be affiliated with a political party when he or she satisfies the grounds provided under the political party's Constitution that indicate

> when a member is deemed to have ceased to be affiliated with the political party.
>
> (9) This Article applies despite the provisions of subarticle 5(1) of this Constitution.

Amendments

Articles 17A and 17B were inserted by the Constitution (Eighth) (Amendment) Act No 21 of 2023. That Act was approved at a referendum held on 29 May 2024 and became effective on the announcement of the results of that referendum on 12 September 2024. The Explanatory Note for the Bill which became the Act included the following:

> Successive Governments since the 1980's have identified that the fragmentation of political parties and the complete lack of guidelines for the formation and operation of political parties and independent candidates are two key factors contributing to the instability of Government.
>
> As such, in order to bring stability back into the formation and operation of Governments and improving the overall governance of the country, a legal and constitutional framework that ensures a strong sustainable political party system is required. The introduction of the political party legislation is a necessity to achieving such a strong sustainable political party system.

A proposal in the Bill to preclude a motion of no confidence in the Prime Minister within 12 months of the election of the Prime Minister did not become law.

Commentary

Prior to the insertion of Articles 17A and 17B, s 2(f) and 4 of the Members of Parliament (Vacation of Seats) Act [CAP 174], which had the effect of vacating the seat of a Member who left the party of which the Member had been a candidate at the election, had been held to be invalid because it was "quite unconstitutional to so hinder such an expression of opinion with the threat of consequential loss of membership of Parliament": *Sope v Attorney-General (No 4)* [1988] VULawRp 4; [1980-1994] Van LR 411 at 5; *Davidson v Shadrack* [2021] VUSC 100 at [28]-[33].

---

18. Electoral Commission

(1) There shall be an Electoral Commission consisting of a chairman and two members appointed by the President of the Republic acting in accordance with the advice of the Judicial Service Commission.

(2) The following persons shall not be qualified for appointment as chairman or member of the Commission –

    (a) a member of or a candidate for election to Parliament;

> (b)   a member of or a candidate for election to provincial government or municipal councils;
>
> (c)   a member of or a candidate for election to the Malvatumauri Council of Chiefs;
>
> (d)   any person who exercises any position of responsibility in a political party.
>
> (3) A chairman or a member of the Commission shall vacate his office –
>
> (a)   at the expiration of 5 years from the date of his appointment; or
>
> (b)   if any circumstances arise that, if he were not a member of the Commission, would cause him to be disqualified for appointment as such.

Constitutional Committee

What became Article 18 was originally included in a working paper of the Committee on "Justice".[65] That was because the initial working paper on Justice gave the responsibility for supervision of registration of electors to the Supreme Court. On 30 July 1979 the Committee agreed with a proposal that the role of the Supreme Court in the preparation of electoral rolls be given to an independent Electoral Commission.[66] The provisions relating to the Electoral Commission remained in the working paper on Justice[67] but were put in the Chapter relating to Parliament in the draft Constitution that was adopted. Following their circulation, the provisions relating to the Electoral Commission were not specifically discussed by the Committee.[68]

Amendments

The original Article 18 provided:

> 18. (1) The general responsibility for the registration of voters and the conduct of elections to Parliament, the National Council of Chiefs and the Regional Councils shall vest in and Electoral Commission.
>
> (2) A proposal for any law concerning the registration of voters or the election of members shall be referred to the Electoral Commission for advice before Parliament decides on it.
>
> (3) The Electoral Commission shall consist of the Speaker of Parliament, as Chairman, and two members appointed by the President of the Republic on the advice of the Judicial Service Commission from among persons who are not members of or candidates for election to Parliament, the National Council of Chiefs or Regional Councils.

---

[65] Working paper E1: FCO107/107.
[66] Minutes at 73-74 (PV25[24]-[27]).
[67] Working paper E2: Minutes at 233 (French); FCO107/108.
[68] Minutes at 113 (PV36[1]); 130 (PV41[2]).

(4) A person shall cease to be a member of the Electoral Commission if circumstances arise that, if he were not a member, would disqualify him for appointment as such.

(5) The Electoral Commission shall not be subject to the direction or control of any other person or body in the exercise of its functions.

Article 18 was repealed and substituted with the version of Article 18 substantially in its current form by the Constitution Third Amendment Act No 20 of 1983.

The Constitution (Sixth) (Amendment) Act No 27 of 2013 removed the reference in Article 18(2)(b) to "local government" and replaced it with "provincial government". It also removed the reference in Article 18(2)(c) to "National Council of Chiefs" and replaced it with "Malvatumauri Council of Chiefs".

Commentary

The apparent intention behind the terms of Article18 is to ensure a non-partisan Electoral Commission. It is for that reason that persons who are or may wish to be political players are excluded from appointment to the Commission.

---

19. Principal Electoral Officer

There shall be a Principal Electoral Officer who shall be a public servant.

Amendments

What is now Article 19 was inserted by the Constitution Third Amendment Act No 20 of 1983 as Article 18A. Article 18A was renumbered as part of the 1988 revision of Vanuatu laws. The renumbering of Articles 18A and 18B as Articles 19 and 20 had the consequence of requiring the renumbering of all subsequent articles.[69]

---

20. Functions of Electoral Commission and Principal Electoral Officer

(1)   The Electoral Commission shall have general responsibility for and shall supervise the registration of electors and the conduct of elections to Parliament, the Malvatumauri Council of Chiefs, provincial government and municipal councils. The Commission shall have such powers and functions relating to such registration and elections as may be prescribed by Parliament.

(2)   The Principal Electoral Officer shall have such powers and functions relating to such registration and elections as may be prescribed by Parliament. The Principal Electoral Officer shall keep the Commission fully informed concerning the exercise of his functions and shall have the right to attend meetings of the Commission, and shall comply with any

---

[69] See "Article numbers in the Constitution" p 3 above.

directions that the Commission may give to him in the exercise of his functions.

(3)   Every proposed bill and every proposed regulation or other instrument having the force of law relating to the registration of electors for the election of members of Parliament, the Malvatumauri Council of Chiefs, provincial government and municipal councils or to the election of such members shall be referred to the Commission and to the Principal Electoral Officer at such time as shall give them sufficient opportunity to make comments on it before the bill is introduced in Parliament or, as the case may be, before the regulation or instrument is made.

(4)   The Electoral Commission may lay before Parliament such reports concerning the matters under their supervision, or any draft bill or instrument that is referred to them, as they may think fit.

Amendments

What is now Article 20 was inserted by the Constitution Third Amendment Act No 20 of 1983 as Article 18B. Article 18B was renumbered as part of the 1988 revision of Vanuatu laws. The renumbering of Articles 18A and 18B as Articles 19 and 20 had the consequence of requiring the renumbering of all subsequent articles.[70]

The Constitution (Sixth) (Amendment) Act No 27 of 2013 removed the references in Articles 20(1) and (3) to "local government" and "National Council of Chiefs" and replaced them with "provincial government" and "Malvatumauri Council of Chiefs" respectively.

21. Procedure of Parliament

(1)   Parliament shall meet twice a year in ordinary session.

(2)   Parliament may meet in extraordinary session at the request of the majority of its members, the Speaker or the Prime Minister.

(3)   Unless otherwise provided in the Constitution, Parliament shall make its decisions by public vote by a simple majority of the members voting.

(4)   Unless otherwise provided in the Constitution, the quorum shall be two-thirds of the members of Parliament. If there is no such quorum at the first sitting in any session Parliament shall meet 3 days later, and a simple majority of members shall then constitute a quorum.

(4A) For the purpose of subarticle (4), days means working days and not Saturday or Sunday.

(5)   Parliament shall make its own rules of procedure.

---

[70] See "Article numbers in the Constitution" p 3 above.

Constitutional Committee

At its meeting on 1 August 1979 the Committee addressed the requirement for a quorum. A provision involving only a quorum of two thirds of the members of Parliament carried the risk of a minority party boycotting Parliament and preventing it from meeting. It was proposed that this could be avoided by a further provision that operated where a quorum was not reached and required only a simple majority.[71] A redrafted provision reflecting this proposal was then adopted on 3 August 1979.[72]

Amendments

Article 21(4A) was inserted by the Constitution (Sixth) (Amendment) Act No 27 of 2013.

Commentary

Article 21(1)

The use of the word "shall" in Article 21(1) and the word "may" in Article 21(2) is not intended to indicate that the calling of an extraordinary session is a matter of discretion. It merely recognises that whereas there must be at least two ordinary Parliamentary sessions each year in addition there "may" be extraordinary sessions if requested: *Attorney-General v Jimmy* [1996] VUCA 1 at 8.

Article 21(2): entitlement to make a request

A majority of members of the Parliament have a constitutional right to require that Parliament be summonsed for an extraordinary session and, provided a request is made, the Speaker may not reject it and decline to summon Parliament: *Attorney-General v Jimmy* [1996] VUCA 1 at 8; *Lini v Speaker of Parliament* [2004] VUSC 42 at 14-15. The possible alternative of presenting a no confidence motion at the next available ordinary session of Parliament does not detract from the right under Article 21(2): *Attorney-General v Jimmy* [1996] VUCA 1 at 10.

The Constitution neither requires nor forbids an extraordinary session to occur on a day when an ordinary session has already been convened: *Speaker of Parliament v Kalsakau* [2016] VUCA 26 at [11]. Whether or not that occurs is a matter for the Speaker and the Parliament.

In *Jimmy v Attorney-General* [1996] VUSC 15 the Supreme Court held that a suspended member of Parliament retains the right to participate in a request for an extraordinary session. On appeal, in *Attorney-General v Jimmy* [1996] VUCA 1 at 12, the Court of Appeal did not need to determine the issue but said that if such a member could not then the relevant "majority of its members" would also need to be reduced by the exclusion of that member. "Members" can have only one meaning in Article 21(2) so that if the member did not retain that right then

---

[71] Minutes 81-82 (PV27[20]-[26]).
[72] Minutes 86 (PV29[1]).

that member would not be counted in the total number of members, hence reducing the number required to constitute a "majority of its members".

In *Vanuararoa v Republic of Vanuatu* [2013] VUSC 102 at 32-33 the Supreme Court held that a suspended Member of Parliament can still sign a request under Article 21(2). However, a Member of Parliament who has not yet taken the oath of allegiance may not make a request under Article 21(2): *Vanuararoa* at 32.

Where a request by a majority of Members of Parliament for an extraordinary session is made to the Speaker under Article 21(2), the subsequent withdrawal of support for that request by one of the Members so that it is no longer supported by a majority does not affect the duty of the Speaker to summon Parliament: *Natapei v Wells* [2012] VUSC 260 at 4.

Article 21(2) requires that members of Parliament should receive reasonable notice in order to attend Parliament and reasonable notice of its purpose: *Vohor v Kalpokas* [1996] VUSC 27 at 12.

The Speaker is entitled to consider whether or not the request has in fact been made by all the members by which it is purported to be made and hence may consider whether each of the members in fact signed the request: *Vanuararoa v Republic of Vanuatu* [2013] VUSC 102 at 31. There is no power to convene Parliament unless there is a valid request from a majority of members of Parliament: *Carcasses v Boedoro* [2014] VUSC 113 at [62].

Where the Speaker concludes that Members of Parliament whose signatures purportedly appear on the request for an extraordinary session have not, in fact, signed the request so as to reduce the number below a majority of members, the Speaker is entitled to decline to summon Parliament: *Korman v Republic of Vanuatu* [2010] VUSC 215 at 15-17; *Vanuaroroa v Republic of Vanuatu* [2013] VUSC 102 at 31, 33.

Once the Speaker has accepted a request under Article 21(2) it is not open for the Speaker to close Parliament while matters to be discussed and/or debated have not been disposed of: *Kilman v Korman* [2011] VUSC 227 at 15.

However, Article 21(2) is not breached by the President dissolving Parliament under Article 28(3) even where a notice of a motion of no confidence has been given to the Speaker under Article 43(2): *Barthelemy v President of the Republic of Vanuatu* [2022] VUSC 158 at [34].

Article 21(2): "majority of its members"

For the purposes of Article 21(2) "the majority of its members" means a majority of "those duly elected and who have not vacated their seat or resigned": *Livtunvanu v Republic of Vanuatu* [2023] VUSC 197 at [3].

Article 21(3): Voting in Parliament

Article 21(3) will be infringed if the Speaker does not allow Parliament to make its decisions by public vote by a simple majority on matters before it: *Kilman v Korman* [2011] VUSC 227 at 16.

Article 21(4): Quorum

In Article 21(4) the expression "simple majority" means "at least one person more than half the members when the total is divisible into two equal parts. If the total is not an even number and, therefore, not divisible into two equal parts, a simple majority must mean the greater of the two parts": *Sope v Attorney-General (No 1)* [1988] VULawRp 12; [1980-1994] Van LR 356 at 4. All counts of the number of members include the Speaker: *Sope (No 1)* at 4.

The transaction of any business of the Parliament when a quorum is not present involves a breach of the Constitution and is invalid: *Sope (No 1)* at 5; *Sope v Attorney-General (No 3)* [1988] VULawRp 3; [1980-1994] Van LR 405 at 2. However there may be a "sitting" even though there is no quorum as on each day when Parliament assembles and the Speaker takes the chair there is a sitting: *Carlot v Attorney-General* [1988] VULawRp 21; [1980-1994] Van LR 407 at 4. As a consequence, a member may lose their seat in Parliament under s 2(d) of the Members of Parliament (Vacation of Seats) Act [CAP 174] by failing to attend sittings of Parliament at which no quorum is present.

For constitutional purposes, whether or not there is a quorum is an issue of fact which may be proved in a way that other material facts can be proved in a court of law: *Sope v Attorney-General (No 3)* [1988] VULawRp 3; [1980-1994] Van LR 405 at 2.

Section 21(5): Parliamentary procedure

Article 21(5) gives Parliament the responsibility of regulating its own procedure. Where the procedures adopted by the Parliament do not breach the Constitution and have been followed, the court will assume the sitting occurred properly, thereby avoiding the potential that legislation be declared invalid many years after the relevant bill was passed without complaint: *Sope v Attorney-General (No 1)* [1988] VULawRp 12; [1980-1994] Van LR 356 at 7.

If the Standing Orders of the Parliament deny constitutional rights to a Member of Parliament then the aggrieved person is entitled to make an application to the Supreme Court under Article 6: *Tari v Natapei* [2001] VUCA 18; *Kilman v Speaker of Parliament of the Republic of Vanuatu* [2011] VUCA 15 at [12].

In *Attorney-General v Jimmy* [1996] VUCA 1 at 6 the Court of Appeal recorded:

> It was common ground that the declaration in Article 21(5) that "Parliament shall make its own rules of procedure" is a statutory confirmation of the principle that Parliament is master of its internal business and procedures, and is not subject to direction from the courts, so long as the rulings it makes are not inconsistent with obligations placed on it by the law from which it derives its powers.

Similarly, in *Vohor v Kalpokas* [1996] VUSC 27 at 13 the Supreme Court said:

> It is not the role of this Court to interfere with the inner workings of Parliament on what at best could be described as a technical breach of its Standing Orders, if indeed there was one, which does not amount to the infringement of any part of the Constitution regarding any of the petitioners before the Court.

The use of the Standing Orders of Parliament to suspend the entire opposition was held to amount to a breach of Articles 1, 2 and 4, 5(1)(d), (g), (k) and 27(1) of the Constitution in *Tabimasmas v Parliament of the Republic of Vanuatu* [2021] VUCA 16. In so concluding the Court referred (at [30]) to the importance of opposition members being able to fully participate in, and exercise their rights in, Parliament.

Remedies for breaches of constitutional rights in Parliament

Breaches of constitutional rights that occur during parliamentary proceedings are justiciable and may be the subject of proceedings under Articles 6 and 53. In *Natapei v Tari* [2001] VUSC 113 the Supreme Court said:

> When the Speaker rules on procedural matters, the Court has no jurisdiction to enquire further but if that ruling interferes with constitutional rights of the person involved, the Supreme Court does have the power/rights to enforce that right [Article 6(1) and 53(1) of the Constitution]. Further, in order to investigate and enforce effectively the contraventions/breach of a constitutional rights, the Supreme Court has the right to examine the proceedings in Parliament and this extends to the actual decision made by the Speaker whether or not the ruling is correct. If it is, there will be no contravention of the members' rights. If the ruling is wrong, the Supreme Court has the power/rights to make orders, issue writs and give directions, including the payment of compensation, as it considers appropriate to enforce that right which is guaranteed and protected under the Constitution [Article 6(2) of the Constitution]. Furthermore, the Supreme Court has jurisdiction to determine the matter and to make order as it considers appropriate to enforce the contravention/breach of the provisions of the Constitution [Article 53 (2)]

In *Kilman v Natapei* [2011] VUCA 24 at [23] the Court of Appeal recognised that it was not possible to lay down any "hard and fast rules or guidelines" as to what may be an appropriate remedy where there had been breaches of constitutional rights in Parliament. It referred to the "important need to exercise a degree of restraint and deference towards Parliament, so that any remedy fashioned by the Court will intrude as little as possible with the continuity and orderly functioning of Parliament".

In *Tari v Natapei* [2001] VUCA 18 the Court of Appeal, in upholding the decision of Lunabek CJ, said:

> As we noted at the beginning the starting point in determining the dispute in this Court, is the Constitution and the rights which are provided therein.

> Standing Orders of Parliament, as the Constitution notes, are the rules of procedure for Parliament. Within Parliament they are supreme and must be

strictly adhered to by all members of Parliament. Nothing in the Standing Orders of Parliament can vary, abdicate or interfere with the rights which are provided under the Constitution.

Clause 27 of the Constitution provides an immunity for members of Parliament in respect of opinions given or vote cast by them in Parliament in the exercise of their office. But that does not in any way lessen the duties and responsibilities placed upon them (as on every other citizen) under the Constitution.

In as much as the Standing Orders of Parliament have an effect and influence upon the Constitutional rights of all members of Parliament, in accordance with clause 6 of the Constitution any person aggrieved, is at liberty to apply to the Supreme Court. Clause 6 provides:-

> 6. (1) Anyone who considers that any of the rights guaranteed to him by the Constitution has been, is being or is likely to be infringed may, independently of any other possible legal remedy, apply to the Supreme Court to enforce that right.

> (2) The Supreme Court may make such orders, issue such writs and give such directions, including the payment of compensation, as it considers appropriate to enforce the right.

This important provision is repeated in Clause 53 as set out above. The Constitution does not provide that what happens in Parliament is to be treated differently than any other breaches of lawful rights guaranteed by the Constitution.

It necessarily follows therefore that the Supreme Court is the body which under the Constitution is charged with determining whether rights and have been infringed or responsibilities disregarded.

To do that is not an interference with the sovereignty of Parliament or with the important immunity which is provided to members of Parliament. It is a necessary consequence of ensuring that all Constitutional rights are accorded the meaning and force which the Constitution itself anticipated.

In light of the above, the courts will approach challenges to the workings of Parliament with caution but will interfere in appropriate circumstances: *Tabimasmas v Parliament of the Republic of Vanuatu* [2021] VUCA 16 at [26]; *Hymak v Weibur* [2021] VUSC 122 at [18].

---

22. Speaker and Deputy Speakers

(1) At its first sitting after any general election Parliament shall elect a Speaker and one or more Deputy Speakers.

(2) The Speaker shall preside at sittings of Parliament and shall be responsible for maintaining order.

(3) The functions of Speaker may be exercised by a Deputy Speaker.

Commentary

In addition to the power to elect a Speaker and Deputy Speaker the Parliament has power to remove the Speaker or Deputy Speaker by a simple majority vote: *Wells v Taga Tarikarea* [2003] VUSC 103 at 4-5.

Keeping a record of the presence or absence of a Member of Parliament is an important part of the Speaker's role: *Weibur v Republic of Vanuatu* [2021] VUCA 40 at [34].

The powers of the Speaker under Article 22 must be read together with Article 21(3) of the Constitution which allows Parliament to make its decisions by public vote by a simple majority of the members voting. As a consequence, the Speaker does not have the sole prerogative to dictate the course of business of Parliament so as to prevent the Parliament voting on motions before it: *Kilman v Korman* [2011] VUSC 228.

Article 22(3) has the effect that the powers of the Speaker under Article 37 may be performed by a Deputy Speaker: *Timakata v Government of the Republic of Vanuatu* [1994] VUSC 3.

---

23. Committees

Parliament may establish committees and appoint members to them.

Constitutional Committee

This Article was proposed in a working paper[73] presented to the Committee on 20 August 1979.[74] It was not the subject of debate.

Commentary

The power of the Parliament to appoint members of a committee must be exercised directly and not by giving the power of appointment to a member of the Parliament such as the Prime Minister or Leader of the Opposition: *Emelee v Republic of Vanuatu* [2024] VUSC 193 at [13], [17].

---

24. Proceedings to be public

Unless otherwise provided proceedings of Parliament shall be held in public.

Constitutional Committee

This Article was proposed in a working paper[75] presented to the Committee on 20 August 1979.[76] It was not the subject of debate.

---

[73] Working paper D1(7) Article 4: Minutes 232 (French); FCO107/108.
[74] Minutes 113 (PV36[1]).
[75] Working paper D1(7) Article 4: Minutes 232 (French); FCO107/108.
[76] Minutes 113 (PV36[1]).

Commentary

Article 24 does not identify how it is to be "otherwise provided". Having regard to the principle of parliamentary sovereignty it appears that it is for the Parliament itself to decide if its proceedings are to be other than in public.

---

25. Public finance

(1) Every year the Government shall present a bill for a budget to Parliament for its approval.

(2) No taxation shall be imposed or altered and no expenditure of public funds shall be incurred except by or under a law passed by Parliament.

(3) No motion for the levying or increase of taxation or for the expenditure of public funds shall be introduced unless it is supported by the Government.

(4) Parliament shall provide for the office of Auditor-General, who shall be appointed by the Public Service Commission on its own initiative.

(5) The function of the Auditor-General shall be to audit and report to Parliament and the Government on the public accounts of Vanuatu.

(6) The Auditor-General shall not be subject to the direction or control of any other person or body in the exercise of his functions.

Constitutional Committee

This Article was inserted as a result of discussions on 15 September 1979. It arose from a proposal of Professor Ghai to "improve the chapter on Parliament, by providing for Parliamentary control of public expenditure".[77]

The words "on its own initiative" in Article 25(4) was inserted by the Committee, reflecting a concern that "the Public Service Commission should be able to act completely independently when appointing the Auditor-General".[78]

Commentary

Section 25(1)

This section provides an obligation on the Government to present a budget bill annually. It is an obligation which occurs each calendar year. The section itself does not require that the bill be passed. The capacity of non-government members of Parliament to amend the budget is constrained by Article 25(3).

---

[77] Minutes 165 (PV49[7]-[12]); Working paper D1(8): FCO107/108. This had been flagged in the Steering Committee on 13 September 1979: Minutes 231.

[78] Minutes at 165 (PV49[11]-[12]).

Section 25(2): taxation and appropriation

In *Union Electrique Du Vanuatu Ltd v Republic of Vanuatu* [2017] VUSC 96 the Supreme Court found that a fee imposed upon the appellant (a utility company) by an Act of the Parliament was valid and that there was no requirement that the fee be paid into a consolidated fund. The Court said (at [12]) in relation to Article 25:

> 12. It is plain from Article 25 of the Constitution of the Republic of Vanuatu that every year the Government is required to present a budget. It is clear that Parliament, and only Parliament, can authorise the imposition or alteration of taxes or expenditure of public funds. Any legislation to levy a tax or increase a tax or to authorise expenditure of public funds cannot be introduced into Parliament unless it is supported by the Government. There is no requirement that public money is paid into a consolidated fund but it is patently clear that Parliament has control of it. In addition and probably because our Parliament is not in continual sitting, Parliament has passed legislation which delegates financial management, subject to Parliamentary control, to Government or to the executive.

In *Union Electrique De Vanuatu v Municipality of Port Vila* [2003] VUSC 139 charges upon the supplier of electricity and water purporting to be imposed under by-laws made under the Municipalities Act [CAP 126] were found to be contrary to Article 25(2).

Section 25(3): government financial control

This provision reflects the long-established rule of parliamentary procedure known as the financial initiative of the Crown. It ensures that the Government retains control of taxation and government expenditure.

Section 25(4)-(6): Auditor-General

The Act establishing the Office of the Auditor-General is the Expenditure Review and Audit Act [CAP 241].

The formula used in Article 25(6) in relation to the independence of the Auditor-General ("not be subject to the direction or control of any other person") is the same as that used in relation to the Judicial Service Commission (Article 48), the Public Prosecutor (Article 55), the Public Service Commission (Article 60) and the Ombudsman (Article 65).

The Auditor General is not a public servant and hence Article 57(7), which governs dismissal of public servants, does not apply to the Auditor General: *Michel v Public Service Commission* [1998] VUCA 15 at 6-7.

---

26. Ratification of treaties

Treaties negotiated by the Government shall be presented to Parliament for ratification when they –

(a)   concern international organisations, peace or trade;

(b)   commit the expenditure of public funds;

(c)   affect the status of people;

(d)   require amendment of the laws of the Republic of Vanuatu; or

(e)   provide for the transfer, exchange or annexing of territory.

Constitutional Committee

The text which became Article 26 was only subject to limited discussion and approved by the Committee on 1 August 1979.[79]

Commentary

Article 26 provides a qualification on the power of the Government to make treaties binding upon the Republic. Because treaties having the character of those listed in (a)-(e) require ratification but others do not, a characterisation exercise may be necessary in order to determine whether ratification of the treaty is necessary. The breadth of the language used in paragraphs (a)-(e) (especially "international organisations … trade" in (a)) is such that most treaties will require ratification under this Article.

Although the terms of Article 26 do not require that ratification of treaties be done by the making of a law under Article 16, that has in fact been the practice: *Government of the Republic of Vanuatu v President of the Republic of Vanuatu* [2012] VUSC 109 at 14. Where that is done, the obligations of the President under Article 16 to either assent to the bill within two weeks or refer it to the Supreme Court applies: *Government of the Republic of Vanuatu v President of the Republic of Vanuatu* [2012] VUSC 109 at 20-21.

Ratification under Article 26 does not enact the treaty provisions as domestic law and as a consequence they may not be invoked before the courts unless the Parliament passes an implementing law: *Government of the Republic of Vanuatu v President of the Republic of Vanuatu* [2012] VUSC 109 at 16-17.

27. Privileges of members

(1)   No member of Parliament may be arrested, detained, prosecuted or proceeded against in respect of opinions given or votes cast by him in Parliament in the exercise of his office.

(2)   No member may, during a session of Parliament or of one of its committees, be arrested or prosecuted for any offence, except with the authorisation of Parliament in exceptional circumstances.

---

[79] Minutes 81 (PV27[16]-[18]), working paper D1: Minutes 213; FCO107/107.

Constitutional Committee

This clause was approved by the Committee on 3 August 1979.[80] The purpose of the provision was explained by Professor Zorgbibe to be "to avoid the danger of a Government harassing a Member of Parliament belonging to an opposition party – this, he said, was something that did happen in certain countries". There was some debate about the scope of what became Article 27(2) and its scope was narrowed from that originally proposed.

Commentary

Article 27(1)

In *Vohor v Public Prosecutor* [2004] VUCA 23 at 14-15 the Court of Appeal said, obiter dicta, that Article 27(1) protects Members of Parliament who are participating in parliamentary debates. It is not limited to debates relating to the passage of legislation: cf *Natapei v Tari* [2001] VUSC 113 and the appeal *Tari v Natapei* [2001] VUCA 18. It therefore protected the Prime Minister from a charge of contempt of court arising from a statement made during debate on a motion of no confidence.

In *Tabimasmas v Public Prosecutor* [2020] VUSC 114 the Court was dealing with an application for a stay of bribery charges against Members of Parliament. It said: "Parliamentarians are subject to the law, including the criminal law, just as every other citizen of Vanuatu. The privilege extended in Article 27(1) of the Constitution does not and cannot excuse criminal behaviour." The statement in *Tabimasmas* would need to be qualified by adding "other than where it is in respect of opinions given or votes cast in the Parliament".

The reference in Article 27(1) to a member being "proceeded against" in respect of opinions given or votes cast in Parliament is to be understood as meaning legal proceedings before the courts: *Korman v Parliament of the Republic of Vanuatu* [2011] VUSC 304 at 12.

Article 27 cannot be interpreted so as to read down the rights guaranteed by Article 5 of the Constitution and constitutional rights of others which are preserved to them under Articles 6 and 53 of the Constitution: *Tari v Natapei* [2001] VUCA 18 at 16.

Article 27(2)

In *Public Prosecutor v Tari* [2001] VUSC 136 proceedings had been commenced on charges of sedition at a time when Parliament was in session. In those circumstances the Supreme Court held (at 2):

---

[80] Minutes 86-87 (PV29[3]-[12]). This debate was based upon Article 10 of working paper D1: Minutes 213; FCO107/107. The final form of the provision is then reflected in subsequent working papers D1(5): Minutes 215, and D1(7): Minutes 232 (French); FCO107/108.

The proceedings were therefore commenced unlawfully and the arrests were unlawful. The fact that the session of Parliament closed sometime during the continuation of the proceedings cannot retrospectively validate them. Indeed, it would undermine the purpose of the article if that were so. The committal proceedings are therefore invalid.

In *Kalosil v Republic of Vanuatu* [2017] VUCA 9 at [27] the Court of Appeal held that Article 27(2) will only be contravened where "the member is required to attend Court or is required personally to undertake any action by the prosecution that could interfere with his Parliamentary duties while Parliament is in session". It does not provide a generalised immunity from being the subject of criminal proceedings at a time when Parliament is sitting.

28. Life of Parliament

(1) Parliament, unless sooner dissolved under paragraph (2) or (3), shall continue for 4 years from the date of its election.

(2) Parliament may at any time decide, by resolution supported by the votes of an absolute majority of the members at a special sitting when at least three-fourths of the members are present, to dissolve Parliament. At least 1 week's notice of such a motion shall be given to the Speaker before the debate and the vote on it.

(3) The President of the Republic may, on the advice of the Council of Ministers, dissolve Parliament.

(4) General elections shall be held not earlier than 30 days and not later than 60 days after any dissolution.

(5) There shall be no dissolution of Parliament within 12 months of the general elections following a dissolution under subarticle (2) or (3).

Constitutional Committee

The four-year term of Parliament was agreed at the meeting of the Committee on 2 August 1979.[81]

Which persons or entities would have the power to dissolve the Parliament was discussed on 14 September 1979.[82] Following this discussion further drafts were introduced resulting in Articles 28(2)-(3) which give powers to the Parliament and the President to dissolve Parliament.

---

[81] Minutes 83 (PV28[4]).

[82] Minutes 161 (PV48[11]-[17]). Articles 28(1) and (2) were proposed in working paper D1(9) and then elaborated upon in D1(10): FCO 107/108.

Commentary

Article 28(1): four-year term

The four-year term set out in Article 28(1) defined as starting from "the date of its election", runs from the date the election occurs and not the date when the results are declared or when the Parliament first sits: *Kalpokas v Hakwa* [2002] VUCA 12 at 5-6.

Article 28(2): power of Parliament

The reference to an "absolute majority of the members" means an absolute majority calculated by reference to the members of the Parliament not including those seats which are vacant: *Speaker of Parliament of the Republic of Vanuatu v Weibur* [2023] VUCA 52 at [18]-[20] (a case decided in relation to Article 43(2)).

Article 28(3): power of President

The power of the President to dissolve Parliament is exclusively contained within Article 28(3): *In re application by the Speaker of Parliament* [1988] VULawRp 17; [1980-1994] Van LR 393; *Sokomanu v Public Prosecutor* [1989] VUCA 3 at 3; *President of the Republic of Vanuatu v Korman* [1998] VUCA 3 at 7.

Where the President dissolves Parliament, there is no power to appoint an interim government as under Articles 42 and 43. The power to govern during the period from the dissolution to the election of a new Prime Minister rests with the Prime Minister and the Ministers holding office at the dissolution: *Sokomanu v Public Prosecutor* [1989] VUCA 3 at 3.

A dissolution of the Parliament by the President is not immune from challenge: *President of the Republic of Vanuatu v Korman* [1998] VUCA 3 at 7-8; *Vohor v Abiut* [2004] VUCA 1 at 4-5; *Vanuararoa v President of the Republic of Vanuatu* [2015] VUSC 175 at [13].

In *President of the Republic of Vanuatu v Korman* [1998] VUCA 3 at 12 the Court of Appeal explained the breadth of Article 28(3) as follows:

> Article 28(3) vests a wide and extensive discretion in the President. There is a heavy burden on anyone who asserts that there has been an improper exercise of that discretion. We are not satisfied that the Petitioners have discharged that burden in the Supreme Court. Where the Constitution provides such a wide and unfettered discretion it is necessary to show that in legal terms the decision taken by the President was irrational and unsustainable. That has not been established on the evidence presented.

In *Shadrack v Molinavanua* [2025] VUCA 1 the appellant submitted that the above passage should be refined so that if the President exercised the power under Article 28(3) then there was an evidentiary onus upon the President to "demonstrate with convincing evidence that his exercise was exclusively in the public interest and not influenced by personal benefit, conflict of interest or improper motive". This refinement was rejected by the Court of Appeal (at [17]) which said: "It is not an onus which is evident from the Constitution itself".

The Constitution does not prescribe the amount of time the President is required to take before making the decision to dissolve Parliament on the advice of the Council of Ministers: *Shaddrack v Molinavanua* [2024] VUSC 384 at [55]. There is no obligation on the President to consult with other parties before making such a decision: *Shaddrack v Molinavanua* [2024] VUSC 384 at [55]. Because Article 28(3) does not set a time frame as to when the President should act after receiving advice from the Council of Ministers to dissolve Parliament, a five-week gap between advice and dissolution did not affect the validity of the President's act: *Vanuaroroa v President of the Republic of Vanuatu* [2015] VUSC 175 at [31]-[34].

The pendency of a motion of no confidence does not remove the capacity of the President to dissolve Parliament under Article 28(3): *President of the Republic of Vanuatu v Korman* [1998] VUCA 3; *Vohor v Abiut* [2004] VUCA 1 at 5; *Vanuaroroa v President of the Republic of Vanuatu* [2015] VUSC 175 at [18]; *Barthelemy v President of the Republic of Vanuatu* [2022] VUSC 158 at [31].

The giving of notice of a motion to remove the President under Article 36(3) does not prevent the exercise of the President's power to dissolve Parliament under Article 28(3): *Shaddrack v Molinavanua* [2024] VUSC 384 at [41].

The exercise of the power to dissolve Parliament under Article 28(3) does not involve a contravention of Article 66 only because notice of a motion to remove the President had been given to the Speaker under Article 36(3): *Shaddrack v Molinavanua* [2024] VUSC 384 at [41]-[45].

In 2023, notwithstanding the advice of the Council of Ministers, the President decided not to dissolve parliament: *Shaddrack v Molinavanua* [2024] VUSC 384 at [52].

The power of the Council of Ministers to advise the President to dissolve Parliament is not subject to the conditions in s 15 of the Government Act [CAP 243] which requires prior advice to the Council of Ministers from the Attorney-General and the Director-General of the Ministry of Finance and Economic Management, as such requirements would be inconsistent with the Constitution: *Vanuaroroa v President of the Republic of Vanuatu* [2015] VUSC 175 at [26].

The power to dissolve Parliament may be exercised by the Speaker when Acting President under Article 37 even though the Speaker is, necessarily, a member of the Parliament: *Vohor v Abiut* [2004] VUCA 1 at 5, 6.

Article 28(4): timing of elections

Voting may extend beyond the day fixed as a polling day in accordance with the Representation of the People Act [CAP 146] so long as that extension does not fall outside the 60-day period specified in Article 28(4): *Wana v Principal Electoral Officer* [2020] VUSC 118 at [13].

CHAPTER 5 – MALVATUMAURI COUNCIL OF CHIEFS

Amendments

The original heading to Chapter 5 was "National Council of Chiefs". The present heading was inserted by the Constitution (Sixth) (Amendment) Act No 27 of 2013.

29. Malvatumauri Council of Chiefs

(1)   The Malvatumauri Council of Chiefs shall be composed of custom chiefs elected by their peers sitting in District Councils of Chiefs.

(2)   The Council shall make its own rules of procedure.

(3)   The Council shall hold at least one meeting a year. Further meetings may be held at the request of the Council, Parliament, or the Government.

(4)   During the first sitting following its election the Council shall elect its President.

Constitutional Committee

After discussion on 31 July 1979 the proposal was for a consultative Council of Chiefs with no lawmaking powers.[83] Parliament was therefore to be unicameral and the provisions relating to the Council of Chiefs were put in a separate chapter. The provisions relating to the Council of Chiefs were agreed to at the meeting of the Committee on 1 August 1979.[84] Professor Ghai explained that "the intention was to establish an advisory body which would be consulted by Parliament. Its members would have no voting rights within Parliament."[85]

Amendments

The Constitution (Sixth) (Amendment) Act No 27 of 2013 changed the name in Article 29(1) from "National Council of Chiefs" to "Malvatumauri Council of Chiefs" and "chairman" in Article 29(4) to "President".

---

[83]   Minutes at 75 (PV26[6]).
[84]   Minutes at 81 (PV27[1]-[14]).
[85]   Minutes at 80 (PV27[2]).

> **30. Functions of Council**
>
> (1) The Malvatumauri Council of Chiefs has a general competence to discuss all matters relating to land, custom and tradition and may make recommendations for the preservation and promotion of ni-Vanuatu culture and languages.
>
> (2) The Council must be consulted on any question, particularly any question relating to land, tradition and custom, in connection with any bill before Parliament.

Amendments

The Constitution (Sixth) (Amendment) Act No 27 of 2013 changed the name in Article 30(1) from "National Council of Chiefs" to "Malvatumauri Council of Chiefs". It also added the word "land" in Article 30(1) and (2) and changed "may" to "must" in Article 30(2). These amendments significantly expanded the scope of the functions of the Council and made the obligation to consult it mandatory.

Commentary

Section 30(1) makes it clear that the power of the Council is to discuss and make recommendations on the matters set out in the section.

Section 30(2) is difficult to interpret. There is a mandatory obligation to consult. It is not clear upon whom that obligation falls. The reference to "any question ... in connection with any bill before Parliament" sits awkwardly with the mandatory obligation to consult. It is not clear who it is who defines whether there is "any question". It may be the Government (or some part of it) or the Parliament (or some part of it). It is, however, clear that if there is a question "relating to land, tradition and custom" then the section requires consultation although it does not define when "a question" will arise.

> **31. Organisation of Council and role of chiefs**
>
> Parliament shall by law provide for the organisation of the Malvatumauri Council of Chiefs and in particular for the role of chiefs at the village, island and district level.

Amendments

The Constitution (Sixth) (Amendment) Act No 27 of 2013 changed the name in Article 31 from "National Council of Chiefs" to "Malvatumauri Council of Chiefs".

32. Privileges of members of Council

(1)　No member of the Malvatumauri Council of Chiefs may be arrested, detained, prosecuted or proceeded against in respect of opinions given or votes cast by him in the Council in the exercise of his office.

(2)　No member may, during a session of the Council or of one of its committees, be arrested or prosecuted for any offence, except with the authorisation of the Council in exceptional circumstances.

Amendments

The Constitution (Sixth) (Amendment) Act No 27 of 2013 changed the name in Article 32 from "National Council of Chiefs" to "Malvatumauri Council of Chiefs".

Commentary

This provides protections akin to parliamentary privilege to the members of the Council. It is in similar terms to Article 27 which relates to the privileges of Members of Parliament.

CHAPTER 6 – HEAD OF STATE

Constitutional Committee

At the meeting on 11 August 1979 it was agreed that the articles relating to "the President" and "The Executive" should form separate chapters.[86]

The provisions relating to the President were finally approved on 14 September 1979.[87] The role of the President and the provisions for appointment of the President had been subject to extensive debate prior to that. In particular, there had been debate as to whether the Prime Minister should also be the Head of State, whether the role of the Head of State was to be ceremonial only, the qualifications required for appointment as Head of State and the involvement of Chiefs in the appointment of the Head of State.[88]

33. President of the Republic

The head of the Republic shall be known as the President and shall symbolise the unity of the nation.

Constitutional Committee

At the meeting of the Committee on 11 September 1979 the minutes record:[89]

> J Aribaud and Prof Ghai explained that the essential role of a Head of State was threefold:
>
> 1. To prevent the establishment of an authoritarian regime led by the Prime Minister, and therefore to have a balancing effect;
>
> 2. To play a role in times of crisis and in exceptional circumstances;
>
> 3. To represent the nation.
>
> For this to be possible, the Head of State required a certain moral authority, derived from his mode of election. It was thus important that his authority should not be too great, (in which case he would clash with the Government) by having too great an electoral base; it was equally important that his authority should not be too little (which would render him ineffective) by have too narrow an electoral base.

---

[86] Minutes 110.

[87] Minutes 160-161.

[88] See 3 July 1979: Minutes 46 (PV15), 10 July 1979: Minutes 53 (PV18), 16 July 1979: Minutes 55 (PV19), 17 July 1979: Minutes 56-59 (PV20), 9 August 1979: Minutes 101-104 (PV33), 11 August 1979: Minutes 109-112 (PV35), 6 September 1979: Minutes 137-138 (PV42), 10 September 1979: Minutes 142-146 (PV44), 11 September 1979: Minutes 149-151 (PV45), 12 September 1979: Minutes 153 (PV46), 13 September 1979: Minutes 158-159 (PV47), 14 September 1979: Minutes 160-161 (PV48).

[89] Minutes 149 (PV45[12]).

Commentary

In *Government of the Republic of Vanuatu v President of the Republic of Vanuatu* [1994] VUSC 2 the Supreme Court rejected a submission that the President could not be sued in any court in Vanuatu or that the President could not be sued by the Attorney-General. The Court said in relation to the powers of the President:

> By Article 33 of the Constitution it is provided that the Head of the Republic shall be known as the President and shall symbolise the unity of the Nation. The Constitution confers on the President certain specific powers which he may exercise on his own discretion (Articles 38, 39(3), 44 and 59(2)), and others which he may exercise only on advice (Articles 28(3), 47(2), 55, 56 and 69(b)) or after consultation (Articles 49(3), 59(1), 61(1)). It imposes certain duties on the President (Article 16(3), (4)). The President does not exercise general executive power – by Article 39(1) that is vested in the Prime Minister and the Council of Ministers.

The Court held (at 6) that no doctrine of immunity based upon the position of the British Crown can be imported into the Constitution of Vanuatu.

In *In re application by the Speaker of the Parliament* [1988] VULawRp 17; [1980-1988] Van LR 393 at 2-3 the powers of the President were described as "specific and limited". The Supreme Court said that the President cannot assume powers or claim implied powers in circumstances where presidential powers are so clearly set out in the articles of the Constitution. As a consequence, the President did not have power to dissolve the Parliament unless the Council of Ministers had advised dissolution as required by Article 28(3).

The President did not succeed to the position of the British Sovereign. Rather, the powers of the President can be determined only by a consideration of the Constitution itself and no doctrine of immunity based upon the position of the British Crown can be imported into the Constitution of Vanuatu: *Attorney-General v President of the Republic of Vanuatu* [1994] VUSC 2 at 6 (approved by the Court of Appeal in *Sope Maautamate v Speaker of Parliament* [2003] VUCA 5 at 4). See also *Government of the Republic of Vanuatu v President of the Republic of Vanuatu* [2012] VUSC 109 at 18-20.

Under Article 33 the President's role is essentially a symbolic one and the extent to which the President may exert influence or control over the Government is very limited: *Government of the Republic of Vanuatu v President of the Republic of Vanuatu* [2012] VUSC 109 at 18.

The powers of the President are those expressly set out in the Constitution, subject only to the possibility of some additional powers in exceptional circumstances described in *Sokomanu v Public Prosecutor* [1989] VUCA 3 at 3-4:

> We would not go so far as the learned trial judge and state that in no circumstances may the President exercise a power not specifically given to him by the Constitution. Exceptional needs may require exceptional remedies. Constitutional law has long recognised that such actions may be justified on the grounds of

necessity… But the necessity must be proportionate to the problem faced. Such a doctrine can only apply in very rare circumstances.

Other than the power to pardon reduce or commute a sentence, the powers of the President are not set out in Chapter 6. They are found elsewhere in the specific provisions of the Constitution dealing with appointment of judges, the ombudsman, the public service commission, emergency powers.

In *Vohor v Abiut* [2004] VUCA 1, a case relating to the exercise of the power to dissolve Parliament, the Court of Appeal said (at 7): "[I]t would be rarely appropriate for the President himself to give evidence or to become involved as an active party in this type of proceeding… The Attorney-General should argue the position and the officeholder should abide the decision of the Court".

---

34. Election of President

(1)   The President of the Republic shall be elected, in accordance with Schedule 1, by secret ballot by an electoral college consisting of Parliament and the President of the Provincial Government Councils.

(2)   When a vacancy in the office of the President of the Republic arises, election to that office shall be held within 3 weeks of the vacancy arising, or in the event of a vacancy arising when Parliament is dissolved, within 3 weeks after the first meeting of the new Parliament.

Constitutional Committee

The manner of election of the President was the most controversial aspect of what became Chapter 6. A variety of proposals were put forward in relation to the election of the President. They included election by Parliament, by Parliament from nominees identified by the Council of Chiefs and election by electoral colleges composed in different ways.[90] The differences of opinion were significantly influenced by competing views as to the appropriate role of the Chiefs under the Constitution. The issue was settled at the meeting on 12 September 1979[91] following "a strong appeal from Professor Ghai requesting all parties to accept" one of the drafted versions. That draft[92] involved election by an electoral college of "Parliament and the Presidents of the Regional Assemblies".

---

[90]   See Working papers C7, C7(2) (Minutes 209), C7(3) (Minutes 209), C7(4), C7(5) (Minutes 210).

[91]   Minutes 153 (PV46[5]). (These minutes are wrongly dated 11 September 1979 in the Minutes.)

[92]   Working paper C7(4): FCO107/108.

Amendments

There is an apparent error in the current reference to the "President" (singular) of the Provincial Government Councils. Article 34 was originally Article 32 and it provided:

> 32. The President of the Republic shall be elected, in accordance with Schedule I, by secret ballot by an electoral college consisting of Parliament and the Presidents of the Regional Councils.

The Constitution First Amendment Act No 10 of 1980 amended the Constitution so that it referred to "local government councils" rather than "Regional Councils". It also changed the word "President" or "Presidents" (of Regional Councils) to "chairman" or "chairmen" (of local government councils) throughout the Constitution (s 1(g)). Despite the fact that the original version of the Article (set out above) referred to the "Presidents" (of Regional Councils), when the 1988 consolidation of Vanuatu legislation was prepared, the consolidated version of the Constitution, which was intended to incorporate the changes made by the Constitution First Amendment Act, included the word "Chairman" rather than "Chairmen" in what has now become Article 34(1).

The 2006 consolidation of the Constitution did not repeat the error, referring to "the chairmen of Local Government Councils".

When the Constitution was altered by the Constitution (Sixth) (Amendment) Act No 27 of 2013 to change the references to "local government" to "provincial government", Schedule 1 item 14 of the Act provided: "Delete "Chairman of Local Government Council", substitute "President of the Provincial Government Councils"". It thereby reintroduced the error which had been removed in the 2006 consolidation.

The error of referring to *"President* of the Provincial Government Councils" rather than *"Presidents* of the Provincial Government Councils" was maintained in the consolidated version of the Constitution published on 29 April 2020.

Given that it is a clear error involving a failure to implement what was required by the Constitution First Amendment Act, the reference to "President of the Provincial Government Councils" should be interpreted as "Presidents of the Provincial Government Councils" notwithstanding that the error was repeated in the Constitution (Sixth) (Amendment) Act.

Article 34(2) was inserted by the Constitution Third Amendment Act No 20 of 1983.

Commentary

Having regard to the terms of Schedule 1 and Article 36, the reference to "Parliament" in Article 34(1) must be to the members of Parliament.

As indicated above, the reference to "President of the Provincial Government Councils" must be read as "Presidents of the Provincial Government Councils".

The Decentralization Act [CAP 230] provides for the positions of Presidents of the Provincial Government Councils.

---

35. Qualifications for election as President

Any indigenous Vanuatu citizen qualified to be elected to Parliament shall be eligible for election as President of the Republic.

Constitutional Committee

The qualifications required to be elected as President were discussed on 8 and 10 September 1979.[93] Although there was initial agreement that the Head of State should be a Chief, this would have excluded women from ever being Head of State as well as other "non-Chiefs". At the end of 10 September there was no consensus on this issue. The matter was debated extensively at the meeting on 11 September 1979,[94] although no agreement was reached. The matter was finalised on 12 September 1979 at the same time as the original terms of what is now Article 34 were settled.[95]

Commentary

The qualifications to be elected to Parliament are set out in the Representation of the People Act [CAP 146], s 24.

In *Government of Vanuatu v Nalo* [2004] VUSC 4 the President was found to have been ineligible to be nominated for election because he was still subject to a suspended sentence of imprisonment at the time of his nomination. As a consequence, the office of the President was declared vacant.

---

36. Term of office and removal of President

(1)   The term of office of the President of the Republic shall be 5 years.

(2)   The President of the Republic may be removed from office, only for gross misconduct or incapacity, by the electoral college provided for in Article 34 on a motion introduced by at least one-third of the members of the college and passed by at least two-thirds of its members, when at least three-fourths of its members, including at least three-fourths of the President of the Provincial Government Councils, are present.

(3)   At least 2 weeks' notice of the motion provided for in subarticle (2) shall be given to the Speaker.

(4)   If there is no quorum at the first sitting as provided in subarticle (2), the electoral college may meet and vote on the motion provided for in

---

[93] Minutes 140-141 (PV43), 142-146 (PV44).
[94] Minutes 148-152 (PV45).
[95] Minutes 153 (PV46[5]-[6]). (These minutes are wrongly dated 11 September 1979.)

> subarticle (2) a week later even if there is only a quorum of two-thirds of the members of the college.

Constitutional Committee

The reference to removal for "incapacity" was added to "gross misconduct" as a basis for removal of the President on 11 August 1979.[96]

The requirements for removal of the President were settled on 13 September 1979.[97] The proposal based upon a working paper[98] was amended so as to increase the number of Presidents of Regional Councils required to be present (from half to three quarters) but also introduce a further clause to address what happened if a quorum was not reached on the first occasion (now reflected in Article 36(4)).

Amendments

Article 36 was originally Article 34. It was amended by the Constitution First Amendment Act No 10 of 1980 and by the Constitution (Sixth) (Amendment) Act No 27 of 2013. The amendments incorporated the same error as to the singular or plural that are described in the annotations to Article 34(1) above. As a consequence the reference to "the President of the Provincial Government Councils" should be read as "the Presidents of the Provincial Government Councils".

Commentary

Article 36(2): removal of the President

This picks up the threshold of "gross misconduct" or "incapacity". These thresholds are among those which apply in relation to removal of judges – see Article 47(3)(b).

Article 36(2)-(4): process for removal

Having regard to the detailed specification of the process to be followed, any requirement to accord procedural fairness to the President is likely to be excluded. The process to be adopted in relation to a meeting at which a motion to remove the President is to be considered is, subject to the terms of the Constitution, a matter for the electoral college.

Articles 36(2) and 36(3) must be read together so that the notice under Article 36(3) must be given by "at least one third of the members of the Electoral College" as referred to in Article 36(2): *Shadrack v Molinavanua* [2025] VUCA 1 at [24].

---

[96]   Minutes 110 (PV35[8]).

[97]   Minutes 159 (PV47[27]-[30]).

[98]   Working paper C7: FCO107/108.

The giving of notice of a motion to remove the President under Article 36(3) does not prevent the exercise of the President's power to dissolve Parliament under Article 28(3): *Shaddrack v Molinavanua* [2024] VUSC 384 at [41] (appeal dismissed *Shadrack v Molinavanua* [2025] VUCA 1).

It is "grossly inappropriate" for a member of staff of the President to request that a motion to remove the President be abandoned: *Shaddrack v Molinavanua* [2024] VUSC 384 at [41]. Although the reasons for this conclusion were not set out, it appears to be because it would be inappropriate for the President to take an active role in the process relating to removal contemplated by Article 36 rather than simply abiding the outcome of the constitutional process.

37. Speaker to act as President

(1)   Whenever there is a vacancy in the office of the President of the Republic or the President is overseas or incapacitated, the Speaker of Parliament shall perform the functions of President under this Constitution and any other law.

(2)   When Parliament is dissolved and there is a vacancy in the office of the President of the Republic or the President is overseas or incapacitated, the Speaker of Parliament at the time of the dissolution shall perform the functions of the President of the Republic under this Constitution and any other law until a new Speaker is elected.

Constitutional Committee

The article which is now Article 37 was discussed and approved on 14 September 1979.[99] Other alternatives for the identity of the Acting President considered by the Committee included the Chairman of the National Council of Chiefs, a person nominated by the Presidential electoral college, the Chief Justice or the Council of Ministers.

Amendments

In its original form Article 37 (then Article 35) provided:

> 35. When there is a vacancy in the office of the President of the Republic or the President is overseas or incapacitated, the Speaker of Parliament shall perform the functions of the President. In the event of a vacancy in the office of the President of the Republic, elections to that office shall be held within 3 weeks of the vacancy arising.

The Article was repealed and replaced with its present form by the Constitution Third Amendment Act No 20 of 1983.

---

[99]   Minutes 161-162 (PV48[18]-[21]).

Commentary

The powers of the Speaker under Article 37 may be performed by a Deputy Speaker exercising the functions of the Speaker under Article 22(3): *Timakata v Government of the Republic of Vanuatu* [1994] VUSC 3.

---

38. Presidential powers of pardon, commutation and reduction of sentences

The President of the Republic may pardon, commute or reduce a sentence imposed on a person convicted of an offence. Parliament may provide for a committee to advise the President in the exercise of this function.

Constitutional Committee

The power to pardon or commute sentences was not controversial. Drafts of a proposed article were contained in two working papers[100] and the final form of what is now Article 38 was adopted from the second of those.[101]

Commentary

The power under Article 38 allows the President to either pardon a person convicted of an offence or, alternatively, commute or reduce a sentence imposed on the person convicted of an offence: *Sope v Republic of Vanuatu* [2004] VUCA 20 at 7.

A pardon has no retroactive effect: *Sope v Republic of Vanuatu* [2004] VUCA 20 at 8; *Sope Maautamate v Speaker of Parliament* [2003] VUCA 5 at 6-7.

A pardon removes the consequences of a conviction so that s 27 of the Leadership Code Act [CAP 240] which depends upon conviction for an offence, cannot be enlivened by the conviction the subject of the pardon: *Sope v Republic of Vanuatu* [2004] VUCA 20 at 9.

The power to pardon may be exercised before or after a sentence is imposed for the offence: *Vohor v President of the Republic of Vanuatu* [2015] VUCA 40 at [27]; *Pipite v Public Prosecutor* [2017] VUCA 13 at [42].

The question whether or not a pardon has been granted is an objective one. In *Government of the Republic of Vanuatu v President of the Republic of Vanuatu* [1994] VUSC 2, a letter contemplating the grant of pardon or remission to certain prisoners was found (at 5, 8) not to amount to the exercise of the power in Article 38.

Where there is an Acting President, the Acting President may exercise the power under Article 38: *Vohor v President of the Republic of Vanuatu* [2015] VUCA 40 at [26]; *Pipite v Public Prosecutor* [2017] VUCA 13 at [43].

---

[100] Working papers C5 (FCO107/107) and C7 (FCO107/108).
[101] Working paper C7 Article 5, agreed to on 11 August 1979: Minutes 112 (PV35[34]).

In *Ombudsman of the Republic of Vanuatu v Office of the Head of State* [2021] VUSC 300 at [25]-[30] the Supreme Court described the power under Article 38 as follows:

> 25. It is noted that the President has complete discretion to exercise the power of pardon under Article 38, and this whether or not Parliament provides a committee, to advise the President in the exercise of his functions (under Article 38). In fairness to the President, he was not provided with the assistance of the Committee which Article 38 contemplated should be established on 31 August 2021 when he exercised his powers under Article 38 of the Constitution.

> 26. As Pardon or prerogative of mercy lies solely within the discretion of the President, such decisions including the pardon order made on 31 August 2021 in almost every instance, are not amenable to judicial review.

> 27. The whole purpose of Article 38 was to allow the President to grant mercy to persons convicted, and that is what the President did on 31 August 2021.

> 28. The power of pardon or prerogative of mercy is not the subject of legal rights. It begins where the legal rights end. It is outside the judicial process.

> 29. The grant of pardon may properly be made as an act of clemency on a national anniversary, or as a gesture of reconciliation to a section of society, or because of the ill-health of a convicted person or of great hardship suffered by that person's family.

> 30. It is not correct to say that the President has infringed the right of one citizen by granting a pardon to another. It is not right to say that in the exercise of the power of pardon the President is obliged to treat all persons equally. It is within the President's discretion to grant, a pardon in one case and not in another if on the consideration to the matter, he considered that to be an appropriate course. A comparison of the nature of offences for which two offenders were convicted is by itself not decisive.

See also *Attorney-General v President of the Republic of Vanuatu* [1994] VUSC 2 at 6-10.

In *Attorney-General v President of the Republic of Vanuatu* [1994] VUSC 2 at 2, *Public Prosecutor v Willie* [2004] VUCA 4 at 2-3 and *Ombudsman of the Republic of Vanuatu v Office of the Head of State* [2021] VUSC 300 at [25] each court noted that the Parliament had not appointed a permanent committee to advise the President in the exercise of the power in Article 38.

In *Public Prosecutor v Willie* [2004] VUCA 4 at 4-6 the Court of Appeal set out information as to how the Article 38 power had been exercised in practice.

The grounds upon which an exercise of the power in Article 38 can be judicially reviewed are very limited: *Attorney-General v President of the Republic of Vanuatu* [1994] VUSC 2 at 6-9. In that case (at 8) the Court was prepared to assume that there may be some cases in which the court would review the grant of a pardon, for example, where corruption was established.

The President may not pardon himself or herself as this would be contrary to Article 66(1) as it would involve a conflict of interest. In *Vohor v President of the Republic of Vanuatu* [2015] VUCA 40 at [23]-[24] the Court of Appeal found that the Acting President had breached the law by contravening Article 66(1)(a)-(d) of the Constitution when he granted himself and others a pardon: see also *Pipite v Public Prosecutor* [2017] VUCA 13 at [22].

<hr>

CHAPTER 7 – THE EXECUTIVE

39. Executive power

(1)   The executive power of the people of the Republic of Vanuatu is vested in the Prime Minister and Council of Ministers and shall be exercised as provided by the Constitution or a law.

(2)   The Prime Minister shall keep the President of the Republic fully informed concerning the general conduct of the government of the Republic.

(3)   The President of the Republic may refer to the Supreme Court any regulation which he considers to be inconsistent with the Constitution.

<hr>

Constitutional Committee

The Committee decided to separate the provisions relating to "The Executive" and "The President" into two distinct chapters on 11 August 1979.[102]

An earlier draft of what is now Article 39(1) which was before the Committee[103] vested the executive power in the President who was obliged to exercise the power according to the advice of the Council of Ministers. This was amended on 11 August 1979[104] so as to vest the executive power in the Prime Minister to be exercised "in accordance with the advice of the Council of Ministers". This was then amended in accordance with a proposal put forward by French and British Ministers at the Constitutional Conference on 18 September 1979[105] so as to vest executive power "in the Prime Minister and the Council of Ministers".[106]

What is now Article 39(3) resulted from a proposal by the French and British Ministers at the Constitutional Conference on 18 September 1979.[107] At the same time, the Ministers also proposed what is currently Article 16(4).

Commentary

The use of the word "vested" in Article 39(1) in relation to executive power is similar to the use of the word "vested" in Article 47 in relation to the administration of justice. The use of this word in both provisions tends to support the existence of a strict separation of powers.

The vesting of executive power in "the Prime Minister and Council of Ministers" may involve some redundancy as the Prime Minister is a member of the Council of Ministers (Article 40), appearing to render specific reference to the Prime

<hr>

[102]   Minutes 110 (PV35[8]).
[103]   Working paper C7: FCO107/108.
[104]   Minutes 109 (PV35[3]).
[105]   Minutes 177 (PV51[2]).
[106]   Working paper C7(8): FCO107/109.
[107]   Minutes 177 (PV51[2]).

Minister unnecessary. However that language may be the result of the history of drafting by the Constitutional Committee and Constitutional Conference described above.

It is not open to the Parliament, by a resolution, to require the executive government to do something. The Parliament must pass a law in order to achieve that effect: *Korman v Parliament of the Republic of Vanuatu* [2011] VUSC 304.

Article 39 provided the constitutional foundation for the employment of political appointees who are not public servants and outside the scope of Article 57(4): *Attorney-General v Kalpokas* [1999] VUCA 4 at 14.

The power in Article 39(3) permits a referral to the Supreme Court of "any regulation". It might be interpreted as applying to any law, a "regulation" which is a subordinate law, or a regulation made under the powers of the Council of Ministers in Article 69. The meaning of the word "regulation" would need to be determined in light of the legislative history (described above), namely that both Article 16(4) and Article 39(3) resulted from drafting changes proposed by the French and British Ministers at the Constitutional Conference, and different words ("bill" and "regulation") are used in those provisions.

---

40. Council of Ministers

(1)   There shall be a Council of Ministers which shall consist of the Prime Minister and other Ministers.

(2)   The number of Ministers, including the Prime Minister, shall not exceed a quarter of the number of members of Parliament.

Commentary

The permissible number of Ministers may be reduced if the "number of members of Parliament" is reduced as a result of seats being vacant: *Speaker of Parliament of the Republic of Vanuatu v Weibur* [2023] VUCA 52 at [25].

The limit on the number of Ministers set by Article 40(2) is an aspect of "the Parliamentary system" for the purposes of Article 86: *Saemon v Tallis* [2019] VUCA 44.

---

41. Election of Prime Minister

The Prime Minister shall be elected by Parliament from among its members by secret ballot in accordance with the rules in Schedule 2.

Commentary

See the annotations to Schedule 2 below.

> **42. Appointment and removal of other Ministers**
>
> (1)　The Prime Minister shall appoint the other Ministers from among the members of Parliament and may designate one of them as Deputy Prime Minister.
>
> (2)　The Prime Minister shall assign responsibilities for the conduct of government to the Ministers.
>
> (3)　The Prime Minister may remove the Ministers from office.

Commentary

Section 42(1)

The Ministers must be appointed from among the members of Parliament. There is no capacity for a person to be a minister if they are not a member of Parliament: *Sokomanu v Public Prosecutor* [1989] VUCA 3 at 4.

The appointment of "Parliamentary Secretaries" on the basis of an employment contract but not exercising executive power under the Constitution was upheld in *Kalsakau v Republic of Vanuatu* [2019] VUSC 60. However the bill for the Constitution (Seventh) (Amendment) Act 2019 which would have provided a constitutional foundation for their appointment was held to require a national referendum and never came into force: *Saemon v Tallis* [2019] VUCA 44 – see the annotations to Article 86 below.

Ministers appointed by a Prime Minister whose election is subsequently found to be invalid are themselves not validly appointed even if they were not parties to the proceedings in which the validity of the election of the Prime Minister who appointed them was challenged: *Vanuaroroa v Natapei* [2011] VUSC 92 at 17-18.

Article 42(2): assignment of ministerial responsibilities

Article 42(2) which assigns responsibilities for the conduct of government to Ministers, and the limit on their number in Article 40(2), are aspects of "the Parliamentary system" for the purposes of Article 86: *Saemon v Tallis* [2019] VUCA 44.

> **43. Collective responsibility of Ministers and votes of no confidence**
>
> (1)   The Council of Ministers shall be collectively responsible to Parliament.
>
> (2)   Parliament may pass a motion of no confidence in the Prime Minister. At least 1 week's notice of such a motion shall be given to the Speaker and the motion must be signed by one-sixth of the members of Parliament. If it is supported by an absolute majority of the members of Parliament, the Prime Minister and other Ministers shall cease to hold office forthwith but shall continue to exercise their functions until a new Prime Minister is elected.

Commentary

Article 43(2): notice

A proposed motion of no confidence cannot be passed by the Parliament except after the Parliament as a whole, through the actions of the Speaker, has had at least a week's notice of the motion: *Speaker of Parliament v Natapei* [2015] VUCA 31 at [5].

Once a motion of no confidence has been accepted by the Speaker and the date set for its hearing, the Speaker is not competent to close Parliament on the basis that there is no business to deal with because that, in effect, is denying members of Parliament a constitutional right: *President of the Republic of Vanuatu v Korman* [1998] VUCA 3 at 6; *Republic of Vanuatu v Carcasses* [2009] VUCA 34 at 8; *Natapei v Speaker of Parliament* [2015] VUSC 92 at [30]-[35].

Where a Member of Parliament withdraws their support for a motion of no confidence after it has been provided to the Speaker, that withdrawal is not a matter for the Speaker but is a matter for Parliament to consider: *Lini v Speaker of Parliament* [2004] VUSC 42 at 14-16; *Natapei v Wells* [2012] VUSC 260 at 4.

It is not a requirement for notice of a motion of no confidence that Parliament will be sitting for seven days after the date that it is given: *Republic of Vanuatu v Carcasses* [2009] VUCA 34 at 6-7. If a motion of no confidence is received by the Speaker which complies with Article 43(2) while Parliament is in session then the session must continue until such time as the motion can be considered and determined: *Republic of Vanuatu v Carcasses* [2009] VUCA 34 at 8.

Article 43(2): motions of no confidence

The effectiveness of a motion of no confidence is not dependent upon the Speaker ruling that it has been validly filed and placed on Parliament's agenda. Rather, Article 43 requires that it be given with at least a week's notice and be signed by one sixth of the members of Parliament. There are no other requirements or constraints: *Republic of Vanuatu v Carcasses* [2009] VUCA 34 at 6-7. The fact that police might be investigating the same issues as raised in a motion of no confidence does not provide any impediment to the motion or the subsequent debate and vote: *Speaker of Parliament v Kalsakau* [2025] VUCA 47 at [29].

It is not a requirement of Article 43(2) that those filing the motion must directly serve the Speaker with the notice. It is sufficient that the Speaker must be told of the notice of motion at least seven days before the motion can be moved and debated: *Speaker of Parliament v Kalsakau* [2025] VUCA 47 at [7], [32].

Where notice has been given of a motion of no confidence, the resignation of the Prime Minister does not avoid the need for the motion to be addressed by the Parliament. As a consequence, it is not open to the Speaker to close the session of Parliament without addressing the motion and allowing the Parliament to determine whether to elect a new Prime Minister: *Natapei v Wells* [2013] VUSC 43 at 11-13.

The right of the members of Parliament to express an unfavourable opinion of government leadership is not given priority over the right of the Council of Ministers to advise the President that Parliament should be dissolved and the right of the President to do so. Therefore Article 43(2) is not breached by the President dissolving Parliament under Article 28(3), even where a notice of a motion of no confidence has been given to the Speaker under Article 43(2): *President of the Republic of Vanuatu v Korman* [1998] VUCA 3 at 10; *Barthelemy v President of the Republic of Vanuatu* [2022] VUSC 158 at [34].

A motion of no confidence will not survive the dissolution of Parliament. In *President of the Republic of Vanuatu v Korman* [1998] VUCA 3, the Court of Appeal said:

> The right which Members of Parliament have under Article 43, is a right which exists only if Parliament exists. It is to allow the tail to wag the dog to suggest that the rights of the Members of Parliament ought to be accorded priority over the rights of the people to elect a new Government when the President, having exercised the provisions of the Constitution, has determined that Parliament should be dissolved.

See also *Shaddrack v Molinavanua* [2024] VUSC 384 at [35].

Once a motion has been accepted by the Speaker and the date set for its hearing, the Speaker is not competent to close Parliament on the basis that there are typing errors or incorrect references in the motion of no confidence: *Natapei v Tari No 1* [2001] VUSC 29.

For the purposes of Article 43(2) the expression "absolute majority of the members of Parliament" requires a majority of all members of Parliament not merely a majority of those who voted on the motion: *Kilman v Speaker of Parliament of the Republic of Vanuatu* [2011] VUCA 15 at [29]-[35]. However, that expression involves the currently elected members of Parliament and does not include parliamentary seats which are vacant: *Speaker of Parliament of the Republic of Vanuatu v Weibur* [2023] VUCA 52 at [18].

44. Termination of office of Ministers

The Council of Ministers shall cease to hold office whenever the Prime Minister resigns or dies but shall continue to exercise their functions until a new Prime Minister is elected. In the case of the death of the Prime Minister, the Deputy Prime Minister, or if there is no Deputy Prime Minister a Minister appointed by the President of the Republic, shall act as Prime Minister until a new Prime Minister is elected.

Commentary

The resignation of the Prime Minister means that the Prime Minister ceases to hold office from the moment of an effective resignation. It is not dependent upon a report being given to Parliament by the Speaker or the acceptance of the resignation by anyone else: *Vohor v Kalpokas* [1996] VUSC 27 at 10-11. In that case (at 10-11) the Supreme Court said: "Resignation is a right vested in an office holder and a voluntary act that can only be unilaterally done. What must be done is to ascertain the intention of the Officeholder. That intention embraces two elements, the subjective intention to resign and some objective conduct which manifests an attempt to carry that intention into effect." Once a resignation has taken effect it cannot be revoked but there is no impediment to the Parliament electing the outgoing Prime Minister for a further term: *Vohor v Kalpokas* [1996] VUSC 27 at 11.

45. Other times when a Minister ceases to hold office

A Minister, including the Prime Minister, shall also cease to hold office –

(a)　when, after a general election, Parliament meets to elect a new Prime Minister;

(b)　if he ceases to be a member of Parliament for any reason other than a dissolution of Parliament; or

(c)　if he is elected as President of the Republic or as Speaker of Parliament.

46. Ministers to remain Members of Parliament

Members of Parliament who are appointed Ministers shall retain their membership of Parliament.

CHAPTER 8 – JUSTICE

Constitutional Committee

The Committee discussed a working paper which formed the basis for this chapter at its meeting on 30 July 1979.[108] As a result of the discussion:

(a)   the Council of Chiefs was given power to appoint a person to the Judicial Service Commission (see Article 48(1));

(b)   provision was made for persons knowledgeable in custom to sit with the judges of the Supreme Court (see Article 51);

(c)   a proposed role for the Supreme Court of supervising the preparation of the electoral rolls was removed;

(d)   a provision relating to the public prosecutor was inserted (Article 55).

A subsequent working paper was then prepared[109] and this was what was considered at the Constitutional Conference, subject to the proposal made by French and British Ministers at that conference.[110]

---

47. The Judiciary

(1)   The administration of justice is vested in the judiciary, who are subject only to the Constitution and the law. The function of the judiciary is to resolve proceedings according to law. If there is no rule of law applicable to a matter before it, a court shall determine the matter according to substantial justice and whenever possible in conformity with custom.

(2)   Except for the Chief Justice the judiciary shall be appointed by the President of the Republic acting on the advice of the Judicial Service Commission.

(3)   All members of the judiciary shall hold office until they reach the age of retirement. They shall only be removed from office by the President of the Republic in the event of –

(a)   conviction and sentence on a criminal charge; or

(b)   determination by the Judicial Service Commission of gross misconduct, incapacity or professional incompetence.

(4)   The promotion and transfer of members of the judiciary may only be made by the President of the Republic on the advice of the Judicial Service Commission.

---

[108] Minutes 72-74 (PV25).

[109] Working paper E2, circulated to the Committee on 5 September 1979 (Minutes 130 (PV41[2]).

[110] See annotations to Article 49 below.

> (5) Parliament may provide for the appointment by the President of the Republic, after consultation with the Judicial Service Commission, of acting judges for such periods as may be set out in their instruments of appointment.
>
> (6) Subarticle (3) so far as it relates to the removal from office shall apply to acting judges.

Constitutional Committee

What is now Article 47(3) (originally Article 45(3)) went through a number of revisions. Prior to the Constitutional Conference the relevant working paper[111] provided, in relation to the dismissal of judges, that they could only be dismissed as a result of a judicial decision, following conviction and sentence on a criminal charge, or gross misconduct, illness, infirmity or professional incompetence as determined by the Judicial Service Commission. The British Government identified that this provision called for clarification as it was not clear whether conviction of a criminal charge was an automatic ground for removal or must be something considered by the Judicial Service Commission. It is not clear whether this was communicated to the legislative drafter, but the clause redrafted at the time of the Constitutional Conference[112] separated the circumstances for removal into the separate paragraphs where they now appear in Article 47(3), tending against any involvement by the Judicial Service Commission in circumstances where there is conviction and sentence on a criminal charge.

Amendments

Article 47(2) (originally Article 45 (2)) originally provided:

> (2) Except the Chief Justice and other judges of the Supreme Court, members of the judiciary shall be appointed by the President of the Republic on the advice of the Judicial Service Commission.

This was amended by the Constitution First Amendment Act No 10 of 1980 so as to provide that it was only the Chief Justice who was to be appointed other than on the advice of the Judicial Service Commission. This had the effect that other judges of the Supreme Court were to be appointed by the President "acting on the advice of the Judicial Service Commission". The making of this amendment resulted in the need to amend Article 48 (originally Article 46), which related to the composition of the Judicial Service Commission, and this was done by the Constitution Second Amendment Act No 15 of 1981.

Article 47(5)- (6) permitting the appointment of acting judges, was inserted by the Constitution First Amendment Act No 10 of 1980.

---

[111] Working paper E2: Minutes 233 (French), FCO107/108.
[112] Working paper headed "Chapter 8 Justice" contained in FCO107/109.

Commentary

Article 47(1): separation of powers

The language of Article 47(1) vesting the administration of justice in the judiciary is consistent with there being a strict separation of judicial power from legislative or executive power. The language of vesting is also used in Article 39 in relation to executive power.

So far as constitutional questions are concerned, in *Republic of Vanuatu v Carcasses* [2009] VUCA 34 at 2 the Court of Appeal described the following principle as "clear and unambiguous":

> Under the Constitution the Courts alone have the power to interpret and determine whether there has been a breach of a constitutional right (Articles 6 and 53 of the Constitution). Neither Parliament, Government or any other persons or body has such powers under the Constitution.

Reference has been made to the separation of powers in the context of decisions of the Supreme Court in relation to proceedings in Parliament. In *Natapei v Korman* [2011] VUSC 72 at 11, the Supreme Court said:

> This Court is also aware of the constitutional separation of the various functions and powers of the state between the Legislature, Executive and Judiciary which concept has been jealously guarded and maintained over many years. It is a role of the Court to ensure that an appropriate separation of powers is maintained and this at all times.

The power of "authorised persons" who are not judicial officers to make temporary protection orders under the *Family Protection Act* No 28 of 2008 was held not to be inconsistent with Article 47(1) in *President of the Republic of Vanuatu v Speaker of Parliament* [2008] VUSC 77 at 27-28.

In *Partners of PKF Chartered Accountants v Supreme Court of the Republic of Vanuatu* [2008] VUCA 11 the Court of Appeal addressed s 20 of the *Mutual Assistance in Criminal Matters Act* [CAP 285] which permitted the "Supreme Court" to issue a warrant. The Court of Appeal noted that the issuing of the warrant was not a decision made in the exercise of the Supreme Court's criminal or civil jurisdiction and did not attract the right of appeal. The Court of Appeal was not called on to address whether or not the non-judicial power to issue a search warrant was consistent with Article 47(1) or an implied separation of judicial power from legislative and executive power arising from the terms of the Constitution.

The power given to the Chief Justice to grant temporary admission to legal practice under the *Legal Practitioners Act* [CAP 119] is not inconsistent with Articles 47, 48, 49: *Malifa v Attorney-General* [1999] VUSC 43 at 12-13.

As a result of Article 47(1) it is beyond the power of the Parliament, by resolution, to require a Member of Parliament to pay costs in court proceedings: *Korman v Parliament of the Republic of Vanuatu* [2011] VUSC 304 at 9.

Article 47(1): hierarchy of sources of law

In *Taiwia v Iamul* [2015] VUSC 168 the Supreme Court held that the hierarchy of legal sources established by Article 47(1) are "in order of priority: a) The Constitution; b) Vanuatu Statutes; c) Substantial Justice; d) Local (Vanuatu) customs, practices and usages; e) Case law and common law." However this decision elevates "substantial justice" and "custom" above "case law" and rules of the common law. That would appear to be inconsistent with Article 47(1) which indicates that it is only if there is "no rule of law applicable" that resort is made to "substantial justice" and "custom". Earlier court decisions and common law rules may constitute or indicate an applicable "rule of law" for the purposes of Article 47(1).

Where there is "no rule of law applicable", the operation of Article 47(1) calls for the determination of "the matter" in accordance with "substantial justice and whenever possible in conformity with custom". It is not entirely clear what "the matter" will be if it does not involve the application of legal standards. In *Assal v Council of Chiefs of Santo* (1992) VULawRp 5; [1980]-1994] Van LR 545 at 9-10 the Supreme Court resolved a dispute about the Nagol jump ceremony traditionally performed on Pentecost by making orders about the conduct of that ceremony in the future. This course was adopted because the Supreme Court considered that it was "seized of the matter" and obliged to determine the matter "according to "substantial justice" and, if at all possible, in conformity with custom".

Article 47 (1): "Substantial justice"

In *Public Prosecutor v Deroin* [2018] VUSC 232 the reference in Article 47(1) to determining a matter "according to substantial justice" was relied upon to admit hearsay evidence from a complainant in the form of a written statement in a sexual assault case notwithstanding that the accused would be unable to cross examine her. Article 47 only permits determination according to substantial justice where "there is no rule of law applicable to a matter before it" and the rules of evidence will provide a rule of law applicable to the admissibility of evidence.

In *Application for summonses to be issued pursuant to Letters Rogatory* (1984) VULawRp 9; [1980-1994] Van LR 90 the Supreme Court quashed an order for the taking of evidence in Vanuatu on the basis that the appropriateness of making such an order was to be determined in accordance with "substantial justice" and that the making of such an order would be inconsistent with Vanuatu's then status as a tax haven.

Article 47(1): custom

While customary law forms part of the law of Vanuatu (see Article 95(3)), Article 47(1) limits the role of customary law in the administration of justice. It cannot have effect if inconsistent with the Constitution or laws made by the Parliament. Where a person has offended against the criminal laws enacted by the Parliament, customary law does not affect a person's criminal liability: *Viraleo v Loloi* [2022] VUCA 33 at [12]; *Vira Leo v Public Prosecutor* [2019] VUCA 50 at [12]-[15]; *Public Prosecutor v Vira Leo* [2018] VUSC 75.

As to proof and enforcement of custom see the annotations to Article 95(3).

Article 47(1): approach to authorities from other jurisdictions

In *Republic of Vanuatu v Bohn* [2008] VUCA 6 at 4 the Court of Appeal said:

> Where there is an authoritative decision of this Court which is decisive on a point, there is no need to go beyond the Vanuatu Court of Appeal decision on that point. The only time that persuasive authorities from other countries could be relevant is when counsel are trying to argue that the Vanuatu precedent should be departed from.

Article 47(3): removal of judges

The reference to "shall" in the second sentence of Article 47(3) indicates an obligation rather than a discretion to remove judges if either of the two thresholds identified in Article 47(3)(a) or (b) are met: *d'Imecourt v Manatawai* [1998] VUSC 59 at 11.

In *d'Imecourt v Manatawai* [1998] VUSC 59 at 11 the Supreme Court emphasised that the reference to "gross misconduct" is distinct from "misconduct", saying: ""gross" is a word of emphasis. It means that the misconduct must be really serious and grave before that ground can be said to have been established." So far as the nature of the misconduct was concerned the Court said (at 11-12):

> Gross misconduct, incapacity or professional incompetence must almost always relate to the manner in which the Judge is performing or failing to perform the duties of the office of a Judge. There may be, in what I would regard as most exceptional circumstances, cases where conduct unrelated directly to the carrying out the judicial office may be taken into account. But that will only [be] where such conduct has some bearing on the Judge's fitness for office. If he is guilty of gross misconduct that has no bearing at all on the carrying out of or fitness for judicial office, such misconduct will not be a ground for a determination by the Commission.

Where the Judicial Service Commission is considering allegations of "gross misconduct", in order to provide a fair hearing it needs to identify particular allegations of gross misconduct and cannot leave it to the judge "to endeavour to sift out of the large amount of material in the reports just what it was with which the commission was going to be concerned": *d'Imecourt v Manatawai* [1998] VUSC 59 at 19.

Article 47(4): promotion and transfer of judges

This is a provision which is related to Article 47(2). These two subsections draw a distinction between appointment on the one hand and promotion and transfer on the other. Notwithstanding the drawing of that distinction, both subsections require that the appointment/promotion/transfer be undertaken on the advice of the Judicial Service Commission. The exception is the Chief Justice whose appointment does not require the advice of the Commission (Article 47(2)), even though it may be a "promotion".

Article 47(5): appointment of acting judges

In contrast to Article 47(2) and Article 47(4), both of which require the President of the Republic to act upon the advice of the Judicial Service Commission, Article 47(5) only requires consultation with the Commission. This gives to the President of the Republic discretion as to who should be appointed as an acting judge. The distinction between the tenure of an acting judge and of a judge is that the acting judge is only appointed for "such periods as may be set out in their instruments of appointment".

---

48. The Judicial Service Commission

(1)　The Judicial Service Commission shall consist of the Minister responsible for justice, as Chairman, the Chief Justice, the Chairman of the Public Service Commission, and a representative of the Malvatumauri Council of Chiefs appointed by the Council.

(2)　The Judicial Service Commission shall not be subject to the direction or control of any other person or body in the exercise of its functions.

Constitutional Committee

The first working paper on Justice described the Commission as the "Judges' Commission".[113] At the meeting of the Committee on 30 July 1979 it was proposed that it should instead be called the Judicial Service Commission[114] and this title was adopted.

Amendments

This article was originally Article 46.

The article was amended by the Constitution Second Amendment Act No 15 of 1981. In its original form the article required the Judicial Service Commission to have as one of its members "a judge appointed for three years by the President of the Republic". As judges were required by Article 47(2) (originally Article 45(2)) to be appointed on the advice of the Judicial Service Commission itself, this presented an impossibility and the removal of this judge from the membership of the Commission allowed it to operate in relation to the appointment of judges.

The Constitution (Sixth) (Amendment) Act No 27 of 2013 deleted the reference in Article 48(1) to "National Council of Chiefs" and inserted "Malvatumauri Council of Chiefs".

---

[113]　Working paper E1: FCO107/107.
[114]　Minutes 72 (PV25[4]).

Commentary

Where the Judicial Service Commission is considering whether the Chief Justice has engaged in gross misconduct for the purposes of Article 47(3)(b) it may proceed in the absence of the Chief Justice notwithstanding that the Chief Justice is identified in Article 48(1) as being a member of the Commission: *d'Imecourt v Manatawai* [1998] VUSC 59 at 16.

In *President of the Republic of Vanuatu v Speaker of Parliament* [2000] VUSC 43, a referral under Article 16(4) of the Constitution, the Supreme Court found that the deletion of a statutory provision repeating the effect of Article 48(2) did not render a law amending the Government Act [CAP 243] inconsistent with the Constitution because the constitutional provision in Article 48(2) would continue to operate even though the statutory equivalent had been deleted.

The formula used in Article 48(2) in relation to the independence of the Judicial Service Commission ("not be subject to the direction or control of any other person") is the same as that used in relation to the Auditor-General (Article 25), the Public Prosecutor (Article 55), the Public Service Commission (Article 60) and the Ombudsman (Article 65).

---

49. The Supreme Court, the Chief Justice and other judges

(1) The Supreme Court has unlimited jurisdiction to hear and determine any civil or criminal proceedings, and such other jurisdiction and powers as may be conferred on it by the Constitution or by law.

(2) The Supreme Court shall consist of a Chief Justice and not more than twelve other judges.

(3) The Chief Justice shall be appointed by the President of the Republic after consultation with the Prime Minister and the Leader of the Opposition.

(4) A person shall not be qualified for appointment as Chief Justice or other judge of the Supreme Court unless he is qualified to practise as a lawyer in Vanuatu.

Constitutional Committee

The original form of what is now Article 49 resulted from a proposal by the French and British Ministers at the Constitutional Conference.[115] That proposal was closely based on earlier working papers[116] but included a provision that required the judges of the Supreme Court other than the Chief Justice to be

---

[115] Working paper E3: FCO107/109. Agreed without amendment at Minutes 181 (PV51[39]) but subject to a minor drafting change reflected in the working paper "Chapter 8 Justice" (FCO107/109) that appears to have been prepared after the Conference.

[116] Working paper E2 Article 3: Minutes 233 (French), FCO107/108.

nominated as follows: one by the Speaker of Parliament, one by the President of the National Council of Chiefs and one by the Presidents of the Regional Councils. This provision became original Article 47(4). The intention behind this change appears to have been "to ensure greater independence of the judiciary". As pointed out below, the provision was removed by the Constitution First Amendment Act No 10 of 1980.

Amendments

The original Article 49(4) (then Article 47(4)) was deleted by the Constitution First Amendment Act No 10 1980 which also amended the related provision in what is now Article 47(2).

Article 49 was amended by the Constitution (Fifth Amendment) Act No 24 of 2006 which deleted the word "three" and substituted "not more than 12". It thereby both increased the potential number of judges of the Supreme Court and introduced flexibility as to how many there would be at any time.

Commentary

Article 49(1)

The jurisdiction identified in Article 49(1) has several components:

(a)   unlimited jurisdiction to hear and determine any civil or criminal proceedings;

(b)   such other jurisdiction and powers as may be conferred on it by the Constitution;

(c)   such other jurisdiction and powers as may be conferred on it by law.

So far as (b) is concerned, the Court of Appeal in *Rarua v Electoral Commission of the Republic of Vanuatu (Majority Judgment)* [1999] VUCA 13 at 7 pointed to the jurisdiction given by Articles 6, 16(4), 39(3) and 72. To this should be added the jurisdiction under Article 53.

The jurisdiction of the Supreme Court includes the power to permanently stay criminal proceedings pending in the Magistrates Court: *Tabimasmas v Public Prosecutor* [2020] VUSC 114 at [12]; *Archary v Public Prosecutor* [2020] VUSC 114 at [7].

In *Partners of PKF Chartered Accountants v Supreme Court of the Republic of Vanuatu* [2008] VUCA 11 the Court of Appeal held that the unlimited jurisdiction given to the Supreme Court under Article 49 permitted the Supreme Court to review the validity of a warrant issued by the Supreme Court itself under s 20 of the Mutual Assistance in Criminal Matters Act [CAP 285]. The Court (at 6) described the jurisdiction as a "unique jurisdiction to be exercised by the Supreme Court in the unusual circumstances of the present case to provide a proper means for a challenge to a warrant which would otherwise be beyond the reach of the Supreme Court". Note that the genesis of the issue arose because the Mutual Assistance in Criminal Matters Act gave a non-judicial function to the Supreme

Court rather than, for example, to a judge of that court as *persona designata*. Query whether the giving of such a non-judicial function is consistent with Article 47(1): see the annotations to Article 47(1) above.

The unlimited jurisdiction granted in Article 49 (1) (in combination with Article 47 (1)) was found to be sufficient to make orders related to guardianship in *Taiwia v Iamul* [2015] VUSC 168.

Article 49(2)

As a Master of the Supreme Court is not within the scope of Article 49(2), the Master does not have the unlimited jurisdiction referred to in Article 49(1) but instead only the jurisdiction referred to in s 42(3) of the Judicial Service and Courts Act [CAP 270]: *Bred (Vanuatu) Ltd v Ngwele* [2021] VUCA 7 at [8]-[12].

Article 49(3)

The terms of Article 49(3) relate to the appointment of the Chief Justice. They do not apply to the removal of the Chief Justice: *d'Imecourt v Manatawai* [1998] VUSC 59 at 16.

Article 49(4)

The only precondition for appointment as a judge is being qualified to practise law in Vanuatu. The qualification to practise law in Vanuatu is determined by the Legal Practitioners Act [CAP 119]. In *Francois v Tompkins* [1998] VUSC 88 a challenge to the validity of the appointment of an acting judge based on whether the judge was "qualified to practise as a lawyer in Vanuatu" was dismissed.

---

50. Appeals from Supreme Court to Court of Appeal

Parliament shall provide for appeals from the original jurisdiction of the Supreme Court and may provide for appeals from such appellate jurisdiction as it may have to a Court of Appeal which shall be constituted by two or more judges of the Supreme Court sitting together.

Constitutional Committee

The first working paper before the Committee proposed the establishment of a Civil Appeal Court and a Criminal Appeal Court as divisions of the Supreme Court.[117] The discussion of the paper on 30 July 1979 only touched on this provision in the context of working out the total number of Supreme Court judges that should be specified in the Constitution. Professor Ghai said "it would be possible to have an Appeal Court consisting of two judges only, even though most Courts usually consisted of an odd number of judges".[118] A further draft of

---

[117] Working paper E1 Article 4: FCO107/107.
[118] Minutes 72 (PV25[11]).

the article was presented to the Committee[119] and the draft was approved.[120] A further draft of the chapter relating to justice was subsequently circulated[121] but the issue of the appeal court was not further discussed.

Commentary

Appeals from decisions under Articles 6 and 53

Proceedings in the Supreme Court under Articles 6 or 53 may be subject to appeals to the Court of Appeal under Article 50: *Naling v Public Prosecutor* [1983] VULawRp 1; [1980-1994] Van LR 61 at 2.

Appeals from the original and appellate decisions

Article 50 differentiates between the original jurisdiction of the Supreme Court in relation to which Parliament is required to ("shall") provide an appeal and its appellate jurisdiction where Parliament is not required to but "may" provide an appeal: *Brysten v Dorsen* [1997] VUCA 3 at 4; *Apriman v Gaua* [2016] VUCA 8 at [13].

Under Article 50 it is for the Parliament to decide if there should be a right of appeal from the Supreme Court exercising appellate jurisdiction to the Court of Appeal. The exclusion of appeals from decisions of the Supreme Court exercising appellate jurisdiction was upheld in *Matarave v Talivo* [2010] VUCA 3 at 7-8 (appeals from Island Courts).

Overturning previous decision of the Court of Appeal

In *Tau v Speaker of Parliament* [2023] VUCA 53 at [15]-[16] the Court of Appeal indicated that it had not yet determined the test to be applied when deciding whether to overturn one of its previous decisions, saying:

> 15. … To our knowledge there is no case in which this Court has overturned one of its earlier decisions in a later case. The circumstances in which it would be appropriate for this Court to do so have not therefore been determined. For reasons we will come to, we do not consider that *Carlot [Carlot v Attorney-General (No 2)* [1988] VULawRp 21, [1980–1994] Van LR 407] was wrong on the question of quorum, so it is not necessary for us to address the circumstances in which this Court would reverse one of its earlier decisions. We leave that for a case in which the point has been argued.

> 16. We indicate for the future that if a party to an appeal to this Court intends to ask the Court to reverse one of its earlier decisions, prior notice of that intention should be given at least two weeks before the commencement of the session at which the appeal is to be heard. Until this Court has settled on the criteria it would apply in a case in which it is asked to reverse an earlier decision, counsel should

---

[119] Working paper E1(3), referred to Minutes 72 (PV25[13]).
[120] Minutes 73 (PV25[22]).
[121] Working paper E2: see Minutes 113 (PV36[1]), 130 (PV41[2]).

also address that issue, by reference to the decisions of comparable Courts on the same issue.

Appeals in relation to election disputes

The exclusion of any right of appeal against a decision of the Supreme Court concerning the outcome of an election by s 63(2) of the Representation of the People Act [CAP 146] is not inconsistent with Articles 49 and 50 of the Constitution: *Rarua v Electoral Commission of the Republic of Vanuatu (Majority Judgment)* [1999] VUCA 13. That is because, having regard to its historical origins in provisions relating to election disputes, the jurisdiction of the Supreme Court under Article 54 should be interpreted as standing as a separate and special grant of jurisdiction outside the purview of Articles 49 and 50 of the Constitution. Robertson J dissented in this case: *Rarua v Electoral Commission of the Republic of Vanuatu (Dissenting Judgment)* [1999] VUCA 14.

Inherent powers

In *Matarave v Talivo* [2010] VUCA 3 the Court of Appeal accepted that it had no jurisdiction to consider an appeal as a result of the exclusion of appeals from decisions of the Supreme Court by the Island Courts Act [CAP 167]. However, it then proceeded to make a declaration that the decision of the Supreme Court was void because of an apprehension of bias on the part of the judge who heard the case. The power to do so was said to arise under s 65 of the Judicial Service and Courts Act [CAP 270] which provides that the Supreme Court and Court of Appeal "have such inherent powers as are necessary to carry out their functions". The conclusion that this section empowered the making of a declaration of invalidity in circumstances where the Court held that it did not have jurisdiction to hear an appeal may be doubted. Neither s 65 or Article 50 of the Constitution provide a general supervisory jurisdiction to the Court of Appeal and the statutory investiture of inherent jurisdiction under s 65 is only to the extent that it is necessary for the Court of Appeal to carry out its function of hearing appeals.

---

51. Ascertainment of rules of custom

(1) Parliament may provide for the manner of the ascertainment of relevant rules of custom except for the rules of custom relating to ownership of custom land, and may in particular provide for persons knowledgeable in such custom to sit with the judges of the Supreme Court or the Court of Appeal and take part in its proceedings.

(2) Subarticle (1) does not apply to any matter being referred to a Court before the commencement of this amendment.

Constitutional Committee

This Article arose from discussions on 30 July 1979.[122] A member of the Committee suggested that, as the Supreme Court would refer to custom in certain cases, provision should be made for a person with knowledge of custom to sit with the judges.[123] This was picked up by Professor Ghai and incorporated into a subsequent working paper that formed the basis of the current Chapter.[124]

Amendments

This article was originally Article 49. It originally provided:

> 49. Parliament may provide for the manner of the ascertainment of relevant rules of custom, and may in particular provide for persons knowledgeable in custom to sit with the judges of the Supreme Court or the Court of Appeal and take part in its proceedings.

This provision was amended by the Constitution (Sixth) (Amendment) Act No 27 of 2013 which inserted the article in its current form. The amended article confined the capacity of Parliament to provide for the manner of the ascertainment of relevant rules of custom by excluding "custom relating to ownership of custom land".

---

52. Village and Island Courts

Parliament shall provide for the establishment of village or island courts with jurisdiction over customary and other matters and shall provide for the role of chiefs in such courts.

Constitutional Committee

This reflects a provision in a working paper of the Committee.[125]

---

53. Application to Supreme Court regarding infringements of Constitution

(1) Anyone who considers that a provision of the Constitution has been infringed in relation to him may, without prejudice to any other legal remedy available to him, apply to the Supreme Court for redress.

(2) The Supreme Court has jurisdiction to determine the matter and to make such order as it considers appropriate to enforce the provisions of the Constitution.

(3) When a question concerning the interpretation of the Constitution arises before a subordinate court, and the court considers that the question

---

[122] Minutes 72 (PV25).

[123] Minutest 72 (PV25[10], [13]).

[124] Working paper E2 Article 5: Minutes 233 (French); FCO107/108.

[125] Working paper E2, Article 6: Minutes 233 (French); FCO107/108.

> concerns a fundamental point of law, the court shall submit the question
> to the Supreme Court for its determination.

Constitutional Committee

This Article reflects provisions included in working papers before the Committee.[126]

Commentary

Nature of the right

This article provides a generally available enforcement mechanism for infringements of the Constitution. It provides a personal right above and beyond any other legal rights and remedies that the person may have to seek redress from the Supreme Court, if any constitutional provisions have been infringed in relation to the person: *Vohor v Kalpokas* [1996] VUSC 27 at 3.

Difference between Article 53 and Article 6

Article 53 is engaged where there is a past breach of the Constitution ("has been infringed"). Article 6 is wider in scope than Article 53 because it may apply to anticipated breaches ("has been, is being or is likely to be infringed"): *Toama v Republic of Vanuatu* [2016] VUSC 1 at [3].

While the power to grant relief in Article 6(2) is clearly discretionary ("… may make such orders… as it considers appropriate to enforce the right"), the wording of Article 53(2) militates against a refusal altogether to grant redress where a provision of the Constitution has been infringed: *Kilman v Natapei* [2011] VUCA 24 at [22].

Live issues

It is not appropriate for the court to determine issues which are no longer "live": *Speaker of Parliament v Natapei* [2015] VUCA 31 at [2]-[4].

Standing

The standing requirement is provided by the words "in relation to him". This means that the plaintiff must be a person "in relation to" whom the Constitution has been infringed, namely "that it has affected his rights in a personal way": *d'Imecourt v Manatawai* [1998] VUSC 59 at 12; see also *Vohor v Kalpokas* [1996] VUSC 27 at 8-9. This provides a limitation upon the capacity to bring proceedings under this section in relation to the infringement of rights of others under the Constitution.

---

[126] Working papers E1 Article 5 (FCO107/107) and E2 Article 7 (Minutes 234 (French); FCO107/108).

In *Mass v Government of the Republic of Vanuatu* [2018] VUCA 11 at [52] the Court of Appeal identified that the general law requirements for standing applied in relation to applications for redress under Article 53. The Court said:

> Generally speaking, unless the claimant's personal or economic interests are directly affected the claimant will not at law have a sufficient interest to bring proceedings. We consider that the requirement to have a sufficient interest to pursue a remedy for a wrongdoing is the same under the Constitution as it is under the general law.

In *Vanuaroroa v Republic of Vanuatu* [2013] VUCA 41 at [23] the Court of Appeal addressed the question of standing of Members of Parliament and members of an "opposition block", saying "There is no reason why people in that category are precluded from commencing or maintaining an application challenging the activity of a Government and its Ministers."

In *Vohor v President of the Republic of Vanuatu* [2015] VUCA 40 at [18] a Member of Parliament was found to have standing to challenge the exercise of a power by another Member of Parliament alleged to have been in breach of Article 66.

The threshold for establishing standing may be low where there is a flagrant abuse of power and severe consequences for the community if the abuse is not stopped: *Vohor v President of the Republic of Vanuatu* [2015[VUCA 40 at [20].

Procedural requirements

Applications to the Supreme Court under Article 53 are subject to the Constitutional Procedural Rules 2003. Rule 2.2 requires a proceeding under Article 6 or 53(1) to be commenced by filing a Constitutional Application in the Supreme Court. Rule 2.4 requires that the Republic of Vanuatu be the respondent to the application. The Court of Appeal has declined to decide constitutional questions in proceedings where the Republic of Vanuatu is not a party: *Rombu v Family Rasu* [2006] VUCA 22 at 4.

Prior to the making of the Constitutional Procedures Rules in 2003, constitutional applications were governed by s 218 of the Criminal Procedure Code [CAP 136]: see *Republic of Vanuatu v Picchi* [2001] VUCA 6 at 4.

In *Mass v Government of the Republic of Vanuatu* [2018] VUCA 11 at [32], the Court of Appeal said that "Articles 6 and 53 do not provide that after an application is made the claim for redress can proceed regardless of well-recognised procedural and substantive law principles that control the ordinary trial of disputed questions of fact and law."

Where a constitutional issue arises for the first time in the Court of Appeal, the Court of Appeal has jurisdiction to address the issue and it is not necessary to first have the matter determined by a single judge of the Supreme Court: *Rarua v Electoral Commission of the Republic of Vanuatu (Majority Judgment)* [1999] VUCA 13 at 4-5.

Except in the most exceptional circumstances, whenever proceedings are instituted against Ministers or other government officials, it is the office which should be named as the party and not a particular incumbent of that office: *Dinh van Than v Minister of Finance* [1997] VUCA 6 at 2.

It is not appropriate to join a judge as a party to an application under Article 6 or 53. Where that occurs the Attorney-General may appear on their behalf and have them removed from the proceedings: *Dinh van Than v Minister of Finance* [1997] VUCA 6 at 6-7; *Francois v Tompkins* [1998] VUSC 97 at 4; *Daniel v d'Imecourt* [1998] VUSC 9.

Role of judge in constitutional cases

Rule 2.7 of the Constitutional Procedural Rules 2003 provide that "The Court is to enquire into the matters raised by the Constitutional Application." In *Republic of Vanuatu v Bohn* [2008] VUCA 6 at 6 the Court explained the role of a judge in a constitutional case as follows:

> The Government submissions were predicated on the basis that there are two separate and standalone approaches to the resolution of court cases. First the traditional common law adversarial approach and secondly the civil law or continental approach which is inquisitorial.
>
> In the twenty first century we do not accept these are separate categories. There is a continuum. It is of the very nature of case management that judges are involved in the control and advancement of litigation. Focussing and fashioning the matter which requires resolution is a vital part of all case management. We are left with no doubt that particularly when there is an unrepresented litigant in a constitutional application (as in this case) a Judge has a clear obligation to assist in getting the matter into an order in which it can fairly and sensibly be litigated. This is not an adjudicative role, it is an ancillary role which is an essential part of modern day docket management.

Availability of general law remedies

A constitutional application should not become simply an alternative means of obtaining justice where under the general law good and sufficient processes are available: *Dinh van Than v Minister of Finance* [1997] VUCA 6 at 6-7; *Benard v Republic of Vanuatu* [2007] VUSC 68 at [8]; *Republic of Vanuatu v Bohn* [2008] VUCA 6 at 4. In *Wanfuteng Bank Ltd v Republic of Vanuatu* [2025] VUSC 285 the Supreme Court reviewed the authorities as to whether or not bringing a constitutional application may constitute an abuse of process where alternative proceedings are available and concluded (at [17]):

> As I see it, the mere fact that an applicant in a constitutional application has other proceedings on foot does not necessarily make the constitutional application an abuse of process. In that respect I agree with the observation in *Benard* [*Benard v Republic of Vanuatu* [2007] VUSC 68] referred to above at [14]. The question that must be answered is whether the underlying reasons for duplicated proceedings being treated as an abuse of process are present.

Strike out of constitutional claims

Constitutional claims are dealt with under the Constitutional Procedural Rules 2003. Those rules include a power at the "first conference" to deal with any application to strike out the constitutional application (r 2.8(a)). The Court of Appeal has also recognised that the Supreme Court has power to strike out an application of its own motion: *Wass v Republic of Vanuatu* [2019] VUCA 11 at [24]-[29]. The Court of Appeal said (at [27]) "the Supreme Court has inherent jurisdiction to strike out a constitutional application of its own motion where the application fails to meaningfully identify a constitutional breach capable of being redressed in accordance with the Constitution, or where the application is otherwise an abuse of process". At [32] the Court recognised that "[t]o file a constitutional application for the purpose of seeking to relitigate issues that have already failed in civil litigation is an abuse of process".

Election/waiver/laches

There is no inconsistency between seeking redress under Article 53(1) and the distinct right of a Member of Parliament to invoke Article 43(2) to remove a Prime Minister by a motion of no confidence: *Kilman v Natapei* [2011] VUCA 24 at [16].

In *Vanuaroroa v Natapei* [2011] VUSC 92 at 19 the Chief Justice said:

> … it is difficult to see how defences of contractual law or equitable principles or remedies would affect the exercise of constitutional rights and its effective enforcement as the supreme law of the Republic in the specific situations and environment of Vanuatu.

De facto officers

Notwithstanding the provisions of the Constitution, the de facto officers doctrine appears to have been accepted by the Court of Appeal. In *Leymang v Ombudsman* [1997] VUCA 10 at 13 the Court of Appeal described the doctrine as follows:

> It is a well recognised rule of the common law that where a person has exercised powers and functions of a public office which involve the interests of the public and third persons, with colour of right, the exercise of those powers and functions is accorded validity even if there has been a defect or irregularity in the manner of the appointment of that person such that the appointment was not a valid one. This doctrine has been referred to as the doctrine of de facto office.

In that case the Court held (at 14) that, had there been some defect in the process leading to the appointment of the Ombudsman, it would have been in the third category of case described in *Re Nori's Application* [1989] LRC (Const) 10, namely an exercise of power "under colour of a known election or appointment" and void "because the officer was not eligible, or because there was a want of power in the electing or appointing body, or by reason of some defect or irregularity in its exercise, such ineligibility, want of power, or defect being unknown to the public". On that basis the request for information made by the Ombudsman and the subsequent application to the Court would have been valid even if it was subsequently determined that the appointment of the Ombudsman was invalid.

In *Kilman v Natapei* [2011] VUCA 24 at [26] the Court of Appeal treated the doctrine as applicable to a case of constitutional invalidity.

Article 53(2): remedies

Article 53(2), in combination with Article 49(1) and s 29(1) of the Courts Act [CAP 122], were held in *d'Imecourt v Manatawai* [1997] VUSC 53 at 8 to allow the Supreme Court to make any orders necessary for it to carry out its functions including, in appropriate cases, the making of interim orders. In that case an interlocutory mandatory injunction was made. The scope of the powers of the Supreme Court to make interim orders would not have been reduced by the repeal of the Courts Act [CAP 122] considered in *d'Imecourt* and the enactment of the Judicial Service and Courts Act [CAP 270], noting the terms of s 28(1)(b) of the latter Act which gives the Supreme Court "all jurisdiction that is necessary for the administration of justice in Vanuatu".

The wording of Article 53(2) militates against a refusal to grant redress altogether and requires the court, upon determining that a constitutional provision has been infringed, to evaluate and grant the redress that it considers appropriate to enforce the provision of the Constitution. Ordinarily it will be necessary to make orders to remedy a breach but there will be rare occasions when no more than a bare declaration will be sufficient: *Kilman v Natapei* [2011] VUCA 24 at [22]. In that case the approach to remedies was described (at [23]) as follows:

> It is not possible to lay down any hard and fast rules or guidelines as to what is or is not an "appropriate" remedy for every circumstance where a constitutional provision has been infringed other than to say that the Court is obliged to consider all relevant circumstances in the case having due regard to the need "to enforce" the constitutional provision that has been breached and, the equally important need to exercise a degree of restraint and deference towards Parliament, so that any remedy fashioned by the Court will intrude as little as possible with the continuity and orderly functioning of Parliament. This approach accords with the respect that the three branches of Government are expected to show to each other.

The common law rule preventing courts ordering mandamus against the Crown does not apply under the Constitution as the power expressly given to the Supreme Court by Articles 6 and 53 to enforce the provisions of the Constitution makes the common law approach unhelpful: *Attorney-General v Jimmy* [1996] VUCA 1 at 10.

The power to make "such order as it considers appropriate to enforce the provisions of the Constitution" extends to setting the next date for Parliament: *Republic of Vanuatu v Carcasses* [2009] VUCA 34 at 9; *Natapei v Speaker of Parliament* [2015] VUSC 92 at [36]-[37].

54. Election disputes

The jurisdiction to hear and determine any question as to whether a person has been validly elected as a member of Parliament, the Malvatumauri Council of Chiefs, and a Provincial Government Council or whether he has vacated his seat or has become disqualified to hold it shall vest in the Supreme Court.

Constitutional Committee

This Article reflects the terms of a working paper before the Committee.[127]

Amendments

The Constitution (Sixth) (Amendment) Act No 27 of 2013 deleted the references in Article 54 to "National Council of Chiefs" and "Local Government Council" and inserted "Malvatumauri Council of Chiefs" and "Provincial Government Councils" respectively.

Commentary

The Supreme Court has exclusive jurisdiction to decide electoral cases, including cases related to the vacation of seats of Members of Parliament: *Boulekone v Timakata* [1986] VULawRp 13; [1980-1994] Van LR 228 at 5; *Korman v Natapei* [2010] VUCA 1 at [9]; *Weibur v Republic of Vanuatu* [2021] VUCA 40 at [32].

The jurisdiction of the Supreme Court is not subject to the constitutional right of appeal under s 50: *Rarua v Electoral Commission of the Republic of Vanuatu (Majority Judgment)* [1999] VUCA 13 at 7 (see also the annotations to Article 50 above).

The jurisdiction of the Supreme Court under Article 54 is not qualified by the power of the Parliament to make its own rules of procedure under Article 21(5): *Korman v Natapei* [2010] VUCA 1 at [9].

If the Speaker concludes that a Member of Parliament has been absent from three consecutive sittings in Parliament without permission it is appropriate for the Speaker to declare that conclusion and record that, by operation of s 2(d) of the Members of Parliament (Vacation of Seats) Act [CAP 174], the Member is required to vacate the seat. In cases of doubt by the Speaker or a dispute by a Member, each can make an application to the Supreme Court to determine the factual issue: *Weibur v Republic of Vanuatu* [2021] VUCA 40 at [32]-[39], [47].

In *Matsamatsa v Electoral Commission* [2003] VUSC 23 the Court of Appeal raised, but did not determine, whether a provision of the Local Government Council Election Rules 1982 which provided that disputes concerning those elections were to be determined by an Election Disputes Committee was inconsistent with Article 54.

---

[127] Working paper E2 Article 8: Minutes at 233 (French); FCO107/108. A differently worded provision had been included in working paper E1, Article 6: FCO107/107.

---

55. Public Prosecutor

The function of prosecution shall vest in the Public Prosecutor, who shall be appointed by the President of the Republic on the advice of the Judicial Service Commission. He shall not be subject to the direction or control of any other person or body in the exercise of his functions.

Constitutional Committee

This Article was not in the original working paper on Justice.[128] The Article was included as a result of a decision of the Committee on 30 July 1979.[129]

Commentary

This provision vests the power to bring any prosecution in the Public Prosecutor. It ensures the independence of prosecutorial decisions by stating that the Public Prosecutor is not subject to the direction or control of any other person or body in the exercise of the prosecutor's functions. By vesting the function of prosecution in the Public Prosecutor, the Constitution impliedly excludes the capacity of private citizens to bring a prosecution.

The formula used in Article 55 in relation to the independence of the Public Prosecutor ("not be subject to the direction or control of any other person") is the same as that used in relation to the Auditor-General (Article 25), the Judicial Service Commission (Article 48), the Public Service Commission (Article 60) and the Ombudsman (Article 65).

---

56. Public Solicitor

Parliament shall provide for the office of the Public Solicitor, appointed by the President of the Republic on the advice of the Judicial Service Commission, whose function shall be to provide legal assistance to needy persons.

Constitutional Committee

This Article was not in the original working paper on Justice.[130] The Article was included as a result of a decision of the Committee on 30 July 1979.[131]

---

[128] Working paper E1: FCO107/107.

[129] Minutes 74 (PV25[26]-[27]) and subsequently incorporated into working paper E2: Minutes 233 (French); FCO107/108.

[130] Working paper E1: FCO107/107.

[131] Minutes 74 (PV25[26]-[27]) and subsequently incorporated into working paper E2: Minutes 233 (French); FCO107/108.

Commentary

In *Office of the Public Solicitor v Kalsakau* [2005] VUCA 13, a Member of Parliament, was found not to be entitled to assistance from the Public Solicitor under Article 56 as he was not a "needy person".

CHAPTER 9 – ADMINISTRATION

Constitutional Committee

The articles which became Chapter 9 were discussed on 18 April 1979 and 25-26 July 1979.[132] Following discussions the articles were redrafted[133] and were subsequently not further discussed as they were treated as agreed. Some drafting changes appear to have been introduced during the finalisation of the draft Constitution.[134]

Part I – The Public Service

57. Public servants

(1) Public servants owe their allegiance to the Constitution and to the people of Vanuatu.

(2) Only citizens of Vanuatu shall be appointed to public office. The Public Service Commission shall determine other qualifications for appointment to the public service.

(3) No appointment shall be made to a post that has not been created in accordance with a law.

(4) The Prime Minister or the President of a Provincial Government Council may, exceptionally, make provision for the recruitment of staff for a specified period to meet unforeseen needs. In urgent cases, the Public Service Commission may, after consulting the Ministers responsible for finance and public administration, make such a decision instead of the Prime Minister.

(5) For as long as their posts exist, public servants shall not be removed from their posts except in accordance with the Constitution.

(6) Public servants shall be given increments in their salary in accordance with the law.

(7) Public servants shall leave the public service upon reaching retirement age or upon being dismissed by the Public Service Commission. They shall not be demoted without consultation with the Public Service Commission.

---

[132] Based on working paper C4: Minutes at 28 (PV7), 62, 64 (PV22), 65-67 (PV23), 68-70 (PV24).

[133] Working paper C8 was introduced on 20 August 1979: Minutes 113 (PV36[1]).

[134] The British Government made some drafting suggestions reflected in a Steering Brief dated 31 August 1979 (contained in FCO107/108), some of which were incorporated in the draft considered and adopted at the Constitutional Conference.

> (8) The security of tenure of public servants provided for in subarticle (5) shall not prevent such compulsory early retirement as may be decided by law in order to ensure the renewal of holders of public offices.

Constitutional Committee

The requirement in Article 57(2) that public servants be citizens of Vanuatu was not included in the working papers dealing with the public service. [135] It was a late addition to the article, arising in the context of discussion of transitional provisions. It was approved on 15 September 1979[136] as part of a transitional provision that became what is now Article 90(3).[137]

The last sentence of Article 57(4) was added at the meeting of the Committee on 25 July 1979.[138]

In Article 57(5), the words "except in accordance with this Constitution" were inserted as a result of a drafting suggestion of the British Government shortly prior to the Constitutional Conference.[139]

The concerns for the renewal of the public service and the need to provide opportunities for young graduates who wish to work as civil servants were expressed in the discussions of the Committee on 25 July 1979.[140] This resulted in the inclusion in subsequent working papers[141] of a clause equivalent to what is now Article 57(8).

Amendments

The Constitution (Sixth) (Amendment) Act No 27 of 2013 deleted reference in Article 57(4) to "chairman of Local Government Council" and inserted "President of the Provincial Government Council".

Commentary

Purpose of Chapter 9 Part I

In *Tumekon v Public Service Commission* [2020] VUCA 35 at [23] the Court of Appeal said:

> In broad terms, it is clear that Chapter 9 Part 1 of the Constitution is intended to secure political neutrality on the part of public servants in the carrying out of their duties, and as a complement to that to secure their protection from political

---

135 The working papers are C4 (Minutes 207; FCO107/107) and C8 (FCO107/108).
136 Minutes 164 (PV49[6]).
137 Working paper R7(2): FCO107/108.
138 Minutes 65 (PV23[3]).
139 The suggestion that the Article would be improved by this addition is contained in the Steering Brief dated 31 August 1979 within FCO107/108.
140 Minutes 66 (PV23[6]-[11]).
141 Working paper C4(2) discussed at Minutes 66-67 (PV23[13]-[14]) and then working paper C8 Article 1.

interference. So much was said by the Court of Appeal in *Public Service Commission v Willie* [1993] VUCA 1 and those comments have not been qualified since. That was reinforced by what was said in *Republic of Vanuatu v Bebe* [2014] VUCA 29 at [25], a decision concerning Article 58(2) of the Constitution.

Article 57(1): "public servant"

In *Attorney-General v Kalpokas* [1999] VUCA 4 at 12 the Court of Appeal said the following in relation to who constitutes a "public servant":

> It remains the position that not every person who serves the Republic of Vanuatu in whatever position thereby comes within the definition of "Public Service". Ministers, Parliamentary Secretaries, the Attorney General, the Auditor General and the Ombudsman provide examples. Critical to the notion of a public servant in the Constitution, and in the definition of "Public Service", is that the public servant works under a contract of service, with the Government as the employer. The office holders just mentioned do not work under contracts of service. They hold constitutional or statutory office, and their entitlements and obligations are created by statute, not by contract.

Article 57(2): "public office"

The expression "public office" is also used in Article 13(3) and 90(3). See the discussion of "public office" in the annotations to Article 13.

Article 57(4)

The reference to "exceptionally" in Article 57(4) indicates that it is an exception to the rules of recruitment outlined elsewhere in Part I of Chapter 9 (Articles 57-60) and the use of the word illustrates that such employment will not be subject to the other constraints of Part I: *Silas v Public Service Commission* [2014] VUCA 9 at [24].

In *Attorney-General v Kalpokas* [1999] VUCA 4 at 10 the Court of Appeal held that the fact that positions were recognised in Schedule 1 of the Official Salaries Act [CAP 168] indicated that they had been foreseen and provided for and hence were outside the scope of "unforeseen needs" as referred to in Article 57(4).

The requirement in Article 57(4) that the employment be "for a specified period" does not require particularisation of the start and end dates of the employment. It is sufficient to indicate that the employment will be for a period ended by reference to a party giving notice: *Silas v Public Service Commission* [2014] VUCA 9 at [27]. An employee under Article 57(4) is not part of the public service, as referred to in Part I of Chapter 9, given that the employing authority is the Prime Minister: *Silas* at [29].

Article 57(5)

Article 57(5) does not prevent the Parliament, by statute, abolishing particular positions in the public service: *President of the Republic of Vanuatu v Speaker of Parliament* [2012] VUSC 183 at 7; *Tumukon v Public Service Commission* [2020] VUCA 35 at [35].

Where a Director-General is appointed under contract for a fixed term, the tenure which is protected by Article 57(5) is the tenure given by the contract of employment: *Republic of Vanuatu v Bebe* [2014] VUCA 29 at [29].

Article 57(7)

Article 57(7) does not prescribe the retirement age, which is, instead, left to the Parliament. Further it is not exhaustive of the circumstances in which public servants should leave the public service: *Tumukon v Public Service Commission* [2020] VUCA 35 at [37].

The Auditor General is not a public servant and hence Article 57(7), which governs dismissal of public servants, does not apply to the Auditor General: *Michel v Public Service Commission* [1998] VUCA 15 at 6-7.

Article 57(8)

In *Public Service Commission v Willie* [1993] VUCA 1 at 5 the Court of Appeal explained the operation of Article 57(8) as follows:

> However the [dominant] purpose of Article 57 is to secure the tenure of Public Servants. Sub-article 8 must be given an effect consistent with that dominant intention. Perhaps the word "renewal" is used in the sense of "regenerate" or "recover (one's original strength, youth etc....)" and the intention of the section may be to allow the replacement of an officer who by reason of declining health, strength or efficiency can no longer perform his or her duties as satisfactorily as he once could but whose conduct does not warrant dismissal.

In *Willie*, compulsory retirement of persons who "would jeopardise the implementation of the Coalition Government policies" identified by which political party they supported was held to be outside the scope of Article 57(8).

Article 57(8) leaves to Parliament the determination of such compulsory early retirement as may be decided by law and thereby does not prescribe the condition of tenure to retirement age: *Tumukon v Public Service Commission* [2020] VUCA 35 at [38]. How renewal of holders of public offices is to be achieved is left to Parliament and it is not for the court to form policy judgements or second-guess the Parliament: *Tumukon* at [41].

In *President of the Republic of Vanuatu v Speaker of Parliament* [2012] VUSC 183 the Parliament had deleted the statutory provision under which Directors-General were appointed and enacted new provisions allowing Directors-General to be appointed and terminated in a different manner. A transitional provision terminated the appointment of each of the existing Directors-General three months after the commencement of the Act. The Supreme Court found that substitution of the provisions pursuant to which Directors-General were appointed constituted the abolition of each existing office of Director-General, notwithstanding that a new position of the same name and with the same function was created. Because of the reference in Article 57(5) to "for as long as their posts exist", the tenure of the current batch of Directors-General was not protected. The Supreme Court also found that the termination of the current batch of Directors-General amounted to "such compulsory early retirement as may be decided by law" within the meaning of Article 57(8).

---

58. Exclusion of security of tenure in relation to political advisers and transfer of public servants

(1)   The rule of security of tenure provided for in Article 57(5) shall not apply to the personal political advisers of the Prime Minister and Ministers.

(2)   Senior public servants in Ministries may be transferred by the Prime Minister to other posts of equivalent rank.

Constitutional Committee

The drafting of what is now Article 58 was discussed on 25 and 26 July 1979.[142] The subject of discussion was the category of persons who were not subject to the security of tenure rule. The original draft[143] provided that "ministerial and regional general secretaries", Ambassadors, and the Prime Minister's and Ministers' departmental staff were all excluded from the tenure rule. After lengthy discussion the Committee ultimately agreed upon ""Senior Civil Servants, Ambassadors" (and Regional secretaries-general)".[144] A subsequent working paper[145] confined this to "the Prime Minister's and ministers personal political advisers" and allowed the transfer of senior public servants. With some minor drafting changes these Articles were incorporated into the Constitution in what is now Article 58.

Commentary

Article 58(2)

The head of a government ministry is a "senior public servant" for the purpose of Article 58(2): *Republic of Vanuatu v Bebe* [2014] VUCA 29 at [28]. The terms of a contractual arrangement cannot alter the application of the Constitution in that respect.

---

[142] Minutes 66-67, 70, 207.
[143] Working paper C4 Article 2: FCO107/107.
[144] Minutes 70 (PV24[18]).
[145] Working paper C8: FCO107/108.

59. Membership of Public Service Commission

(1)   The Public Service Commission shall be composed of five members appointed for 3 years by the President of the Republic after consultation with the Prime Minister.

(2)   The President of the Republic shall appoint every year, from among the members of the Commission, a chairman who shall be responsible for organising its proceedings.

(3)   A person shall be disqualified for appointment as a member of the Commission if he is a member of Parliament, the Malvatumauri Council of Chiefs or a Provincial Government Council or if he exercises a position of responsibility within a political party.

(4)   A person shall cease to be a member of the Commission if circumstances arise that, if he were not a member, would disqualify him for appointment as such.

Constitutional Committee

On 25 July 1979 the Committee decided that the Public Service Commission should have five members, that should be appointed at the same time and for the same term of office.[146]

Article 59(4) was incorporated as a result of a drafting suggestion by the British Government shortly prior to the Constitutional Conference.[147]

Amendments

The Constitution First Amendment Act No 10 of 1980 and the Constitution (Sixth) (Amendment) Act No 27 of 2013 resulted in the Article referring to Provincial Government Councils rather than Local Government Councils or Regional Councils.

The Constitution (Sixth) (Amendment) Act No 27 of 2013 deleted the reference in Article 59(3) to "National Council of Chiefs" and inserted "Malvatumauri Council of Chiefs".

Commentary

Article 59(4)

The word "arise" in Article 59(4) is an elastic term that encompasses the situation where a disqualifying circumstance only comes to light or becomes known after a member's appointment: *Michel v President of the Republic of Vanuatu* [2015] VUCA

---

[146]   Minutes 67 (PV23[17]).

[147]   The suggestion that this was a corollary of the qualifications for membership (now Article 59(3)) is contained in the Steering Brief dated 31 August 1979 within FCO107/108.

14 at [13]. It appears that in that case the Court of Appeal accepted that the circumstances that might disqualify a person from appointment included a failure to meet qualifications for appointment set out in the Public Service Act [CAP 246] and was not limited to the disqualifying circumstances set out in Article 59(3).

---

60. Functions of Public Service Commission

(1)   The Public Service Commission shall be responsible for the appointment and promotion of public servants, and the selection of those to undergo training courses in Vanuatu or overseas. For such purposes it may organise competitive examinations.

(2)   The Commission shall also be responsible for the discipline of public servants.

(3)   The Commission shall have no authority over the members of the judiciary, the armed forces, the police and the teaching services.

(4)   The Commission shall not be subject to the direction or control of any other person or body in the exercise of its functions.

Constitutional Committee

Article 60(1) was re-drafted by the legislative draftsman shortly prior to the Constitutional Conference to make it clear that the Public Service Commission was responsible for "appointment" of public servants. The relevant working paper of the Committee[148] had indicated that it had the function to "recruit" public servants but this was arguably uncertain as to who actually appointed public servants.[149]

The relevant working paper of the Committee[150] referred to the Public Service Commission recruiting "the State's and the Regions' public servants" but the final form of the Article approved at the Constitutional Conference and now reflected in Article 60(1) simply refers to "public servants".

In the original working paper dealing with this subject, the exclusion in what is now Article 60(3) was "Judges, Police and teaching services".[151] This working paper was discussed at the meeting on 25 July 1979 and the minutes record: "The Committee also approved that there should be separate Commissions for Teachers, Police and the Judiciary".[152] In a second working paper addressing this subject, the scope of the exclusion from the functions of the Public Service

---

[148]   Working paper C8: FCO107/108.

[149]   The issue was raised in the British Government Steering Brief dated 31 August 1979: FCO107/108.

[150]   Working paper C8, Article 4.

[151]   Working paper C4 Article 4: Minutes 207; FCO107/107.

[152]   Minutes at 67 (PV23[17]).

Commission was changed to "Judicial Service Commission, the armed forces, the Police and the teaching services".[153]

What is now Article 60(4) was incorporated by the legislative draftsman shortly prior to the Constitutional Conference at the suggestion of the British Government. The position of the British Government was that "if the Commission is to be independent, it would be as well to say so" and suggested the language now incorporated in Article 60(4).[154]

Commentary

Article 60(1): Temporary appointments

Under Article 60(1), the functions of the Public Service Commission relating to "the appointment and promotion of public servants" do not extend to temporary appointments arising from the absence of officeholders for proper reasons. The Commission is responsible for permanent appointments and permanent promotions: *Nixon v Republic of Vanuatu* [2004] VUSC 71 at 8.

Article 60(3)

In *Teaching Service Commission v Director General Ministry of Education and Training* [2023] VUSC 252 the Supreme Court confined the reference to "the teaching services" to teachers as distinct from the Teaching Service Commission, saying (at [37]):

> By saying the PSC has no authority over the "teaching services", Article 60(3) of the Constitution makes a distinction between the teaching services, i.e. the teachers, and the Teaching Service Commission, which is an agency of government. Section 36 of the Public Service Act defines disciplinary matters. It applies to employees as defined in s 5. I do not therefore consider there is a serious question to be tried with respect to the second and third applications which concern the PSC's engagement with employees as defined in the Public Service Act.

The Auditor General is not in the list of exclusions in Article 60(3) because the Auditor General is not a public servant for the purposes of this part of the Constitution: *Michel v Public Service Commission* [1998] VUCA 15 at 7.

Article 60(4)

The formula used in Article 60(4) in relation to the independence of the Public Service Commission ("not be subject to the direction or control of any other person") is the same as that used in relation to the Auditor-General (Article 25), the Judicial Service Commission (Article 48), the Public Prosecutor (Article 55) and the Ombudsman (Article 65).

---

[153] Working paper C8 Article 4.
[154] See the Steering Brief dated 31 August 1979 within FCO107/108.

Article 60(4) is intended to protect the Public Service Commission from outside interference. It is not intended to prevent either courts or the Parliament from exercising their respective powers in a way which would affect the Commission in the exercise of its functions: *Public Service Commission v Willie* [1993] VUCA 1 at 4. It does not have the effect of preventing a court directing a prerogative writ to the Commission: *Taurakoto v Batic* [1993] VULawRp 4; [1980-1994] Van LR 620 at 15.

In *President of the Republic of Vanuatu v Speaker of Parliament* [2000] VUSC 43, a referral under Article 16(4) of the Constitution, the Supreme Court found that the deletion of a statutory provision which repeated the effect of Article 60(4) did not render a law amending the Government Act inconsistent with the Constitution because the constitutional provision in Article 60(4) would continue to operate even though the statutory equivalent had been deleted.

Part II – The Ombudsman

61. Ombudsman

(1)   The Ombudsman shall be appointed, for 5 years, by the President of the Republic after consultation with the Prime Minister, the Speaker of Parliament, the leaders of the political parties represented in Parliament, the President of the Malvatumauri Council of Chiefs, the Presidents of the Provincial Government Councils, and the chairmen of the Public Service Commission and the Judicial Service Commission.

(2)   A person shall be disqualified for appointment as Ombudsman if he is a member of Parliament, the Malvatumauri Council of Chiefs or a Provincial Government Council, if he holds any other public office, or if he exercises a position of responsibility within a political party.

(3)   A person shall cease to be Ombudsman if circumstances arise that, if he were not the Ombudsman, would disqualify him for appointment as such.

Constitutional Committee

The proposal to establish an ombudsman[155] was discussed at the meeting of the Committee on 26 July 1979.[156] The proposal was for an office named the "Mediator of the New Hebrides" but, by the time it was discussed by the Committee, the office was referred to as the Ombudsman. The proposal included Articles 5, 6, 7 which are now generally reflected in Articles 61, 62, 63. No member of the Committee objected to the principle of having an ombudsman.[157]

---

[155] Working paper C4: Minutes 207; FCO107/107.
[156] Minutes 68-70 (PV24).
[157] Minutes 69 (PV24[4]).

Article 61(3) was included by the legislative draftsman shortly prior to the Constitutional Conference at the suggestion of the British Government.[158] A similar amendment involved the inclusion of Article 59(4).

Amendments

The Constitution (Sixth) (Amendment) Act No 27 of 2013 deleted the reference in Article 61(1) to "chairmen of Local Government Councils" and inserted "Presidents of the Provincial Government Councils". It also deleted "chairman of the National Council of Chiefs" and inserted "President of the Malvatumauri Council of Chiefs". In Article 61(2) it deleted references to the "National Council of Chiefs" and "Local Government Council" and inserted in their place references to "Malvatumauri Council of Chiefs" and "Provincial Government Council".

Commentary

Part II of Chapter 9 is not a code that would exclude the power of the Parliament to make a law relating to the Ombudsman: *Virelala v Ombudsman* [1997] VUSC 35 at 26. The Ombudsman Act No 27 of 1998 was found to be valid in *Ombudsman v Batick* [2001] VUSC 45 at 20. The earlier Ombudsman Act No 14 of 1995 had been found to be valid except in one minor respect in *Virelala v Ombudsman* [1997] VUSC 35.

In *Ombudsman v Attorney-General* [1997] VUSC 41 the Supreme Court declared that a decision of the Council of Ministers to draft a petition seeking the dismissal of the Ombudsman was without a legal basis and of no effect where that was inconsistent with the provisions of Article 61 and s 9 of the Ombudsman Act No 14 of 1995.

In *President of the Republic of Vanuatu v Attorney-General* [1998] VUSC 18 the repeal of the Ombudsman Act No 14 of 1995 was not found to be inconsistent with the Constitution. A replacement Act was subsequently passed: Ombudsman Act No 27 of 1998.

---

62. Enquiries by Ombudsman

(1)   The Ombudsman may enquire into the conduct of any person or body to which this Article applies –

    (a)   upon receiving a complaint from a member of the public (or, if for reasons of incapacity, from his representative or a member of his family) who claims to have been the victim of an injustice as a result of particular conduct;

---

[158] The suggestion was raised in the British Government Steering Brief dated 31 August 1979: FCO107/108.

> (b)   at the request of a Minister, a member of Parliament, of the Malvatumauri Council of Chiefs or of a Provincial Government Council; or
>
> (c)   of his own initiative.
>
> (2) This Article shall apply to all public servants, public authorities and ministerial departments, with the exception of the President of the Republic, the Judicial Service Commission, the Supreme Court and other judicial bodies.
>
> (3) The Ombudsman may request any Minister, public servant, administrator, authority concerned or any person likely to assist him, to furnish him with information and documents needed for his enquiry.
>
> (4) The Ombudsman shall grant the person or body complained of an opportunity to reply to the complaints made against them.
>
> (5) The enquiries of the Ombudsman shall be conducted in private.

Constitutional Committee

A working paper before the Committee[159] proposed that the "Civil Service Commission" be amongst the bodies listed in Article 62(2) which were excluded from investigation by the Ombudsman. However, the Committee decided to remove the reference to the Civil Service Commission on 26 July 1979.[160]

Amendments

The Constitution (Sixth) (Amendment) Act No 27 of 2013 deleted the references in Article 62(1)(b) to "National Council of Chiefs" and "Local Government Council" and inserted in their place references to "Malvatumauri Council of Chiefs" and "Provincial Government Council" respectively.

Commentary

The Ombudsman does not have standing to challenge the exercise of the pardoning power under Article 38 of the Constitution by the President as Article 62(2) excludes the President from the powers of the Ombudsman to undertake enquiries, and the exercise of the pardoning power in relation to one citizen does not affect the rights of another: *Ombudsman of the Republic of Vanuatu v Office of the Head of State* [2021] VUSC 300 at [18]-[20], [30].

Given that the powers of enquiry and reporting arise from the Constitution, the provisions of the Ombudsman Act [CAP 252] prevail over the Official Secrets Act [CAP 111]: *Ombudsman v Kombe* [1998] VUSC 3.

---

[159] Working paper C4: Minutes 207; FCO107/107.
[160] Minutes 69 (PV24[6]).

Article 62(1)

As the terms of Article 62(1)(c) make clear, the power of the Ombudsman to conduct an enquiry is not dependent upon a complaint from an individual: *Leymang v Ombudsman* [1997] VUCA 10 at 16.

Article 62(2)

A provision of the Ombudsman Act No 14 of 1995 which permitted the President to enquire into the conduct of a person holding judicial office and to delegate that power of enquiry to the Ombudsman was found to be contrary to Article 62(2) and hence invalid: *Virelala v Ombudsman* [1997] VUSC 35 at 28-29. That was because Article 62(2) excluded from the Ombudsman's power of enquiry "the Supreme Court and other judicial bodies".

Article 62(3)

The entitlement in Article 62(3) to request information and documents is supplemented by s 22-23 of the Ombudsman Act [CAP 252].

The fact that information was communicated in confidence does not provide a basis for refusing to provide information requested by the Ombudsman: *Leymang v Ombudsman* [1997] VUCA 10 at 25.

Article 62(4)

The obligation upon the Ombudsman under Article 62(4) to give a person "an opportunity to reply to the complaints made against them" involves giving the person a reasonable time in which to do so and a failure to afford reasonable time taking account of all of the surrounding circumstances would be tantamount to a failure to grant "an opportunity to reply" within the terms of the Constitution: *Jimmy v Ombudsman* [1996] VUSC 26 at 8-9.

The obligation in Article 62(4) requires that the opportunity to reply to the "complaints" occurs before the Ombudsman has come to any decision. That does not prevent the Ombudsman from starting an enquiry after receiving complaints about a party and there is no procedural unfairness in the Ombudsman deciding to embark on an enquiry and continuing the enquiry while requesting a reply to the complaints: *Jimmy v Ombudsman* [1996] VUSC 26 at 8-9.

63. Findings of the Ombudsman and reports

(1)   Wherever, after due enquiry, the Ombudsman concludes that a complaint is unjustified, he shall so inform the complainant and the Prime Minister and the head of the public department or authority concerned.

(2)   Wherever, after due enquiry, the Ombudsman concludes that conduct was contrary to the law, based on error of law or of fact, delayed for unjustified reasons, or unjust or blatantly unreasonable and that, consequently, any decision taken should be annulled or changed or that any practice followed should be revised, he shall forward his findings to

the Prime Minister and to the head of the public authority or department directly concerned.

(3)   The report of the Ombudsman shall be public unless he decides to keep the report, or parts of it, confidential to the Prime Minister and the person in charge of the relevant public service, on the grounds of public security or public interest. The complainant shall in any case be told of the findings of the Ombudsman.

(4)   The Prime Minister or the person in charge of the relevant public service shall decide upon the findings of the Ombudsman within a reasonable time and the decision, with reasons, shall be given to the complainant forthwith. Any period limiting the time in which legal proceedings may be commenced shall not begin to run until the complainant has received the decision.

(5)   The Ombudsman shall present a general report to Parliament each year and may make such additional reports as he considers necessary concerning the discharge of his functions and action taken or his findings. He may draw the attention of Parliament to any defects which appear to him to exist in the administration.

Constitutional Committee

On 26 July 1979 the Committee discussed whether reports of the Ombudsman should be confidential and what should occur if the relevant Minister had not responded to an Ombudsman's report within a reasonable time. This led to Professors Zorgbibe and Ghai redrafting the proposed Article.[161] The revised article maintained the confidential nature of reports but permitted the Ombudsman to provide to the National Assembly "such additional reports as he may consider necessary".[162] That is now reflected in Article 63(5).

On 15 September 1979 the Committee adopted Professor Ghai's proposal that the Ombudsman have discretion to publish a report and to require the complainant to be told of the government's decision in relation to the findings of the Ombudsman.[163] Professor Ghai explained that the expression "reasonable time" in what became Article 63(4) was better than a fixed time "as different situations would require different reactions from the Government".[164]

In Article 63(4) the provision relating to limitation periods went through a number of drafts. It was not contained in the first working paper on the

---

[161] Minutes 69-70 (PV24[8]-[13]).

[162] Minutes 70 (PV24[15]).

[163] Minutes 165 (PV49[13]-[15]).

[164] Minutes 165; (PV49[14]).

subject.[165] The second working paper[166] provided: "The period of limitation for the institution of proceedings in the Supreme Court shall run from the date of the rejection, whether implicit or explicit of the Ombudsman's findings". The British Government identified that the clause should be clarified so as to make it clear that what it referred to was any proceedings in the Supreme Court "that may be available in respect of the action complained of".[167] The next working paper[168] provided: "The period of limitation for legal suit will not begin to run until the complainant has received the decision". The language ultimately adopted was: "Any period limiting the time in which legal proceedings may be commenced shall not begin to run until the complainant has received the decision."

64. Right of a citizen to services in own language

(1)   A citizen of Vanuatu may obtain, in the official language that he uses, the services which he may rightfully expect from the administration of the Republic of Vanuatu.

(2)   Where a citizen considers that there has been a breach of subarticle (1) he may make a complaint to the Ombudsman who shall conduct an enquiry in accordance with Articles 62 and 63.

(3)   The Ombudsman shall, each year, make a special report to Parliament concerning the observance of multilingualism and the measures likely to ensure its respect.

Constitutional Committee

On 26 July 1979 a proposal for a provision to the effect of what is now Article 64 contained in a working paper[169] was discussed. Professor Zorgbibe explained that although such task could be given to a commission, it was more efficient for the Ombudsman to have this role.[170]

The Article was included in a second working paper of the Committee on the topic[171] and then included with minor drafting revisions as what has become Article 64.

---

[165] Working paper C4: Minutes 208; FCO107/107.

[166] Working paper C8: FCO107/108.

[167] This is contained in the Steering Brief dated 31 August 1979 in FCO107/108. It is not clear whether the suggestion was communicated or whether it was overtaken by the presentation of working paper C8(2).

[168] Working paper C8(2) (Minutes 211 (FCO107/108)) distributed and approved 15 September 1979: Minutes at 164, 165 (PV49[1], [15]).

[169] Working paper C4: Minutes 208; FCO107/107.

[170] Minutes 70 (PV24[6]).

[171] Working paper C8 Article 8: FCO107/108.

---

65. Ombudsman not subject to direction or control

The Ombudsman shall not be subject to the direction or control of any other person or body in the exercise of his functions.

Constitutional Committee

What is now Article 65 was included by the legislative draftsman shortly prior to the Constitutional Conference at the suggestion of the British Government in order to remove any doubt about the independence of the Ombudsman.[172]

Commentary

The formula used in Article 65 in relation to the independence of the Ombudsman ("not be subject to the direction or control of any other person") is the same as that used in relation to the Auditor-General (Article 25), the Judicial Service Commission (Article 48), the Public Prosecutor (Article 55) and the Public Service Commission (Article 60).

Article 65 must be understood to mean that the Ombudsman shall not be subject to direction or control of any other person in the lawful performance of the powers which arise under Article 61-63 of the Constitution. If the lawful performance of those powers is exceeded the Ombudsman is subject to restraint by the Supreme Court: *Leymang v Ombudsman* [1997] VUCA 10 at 21.

---

[172] The suggested drafting change is contained in the Steering Brief dated 31 August 1979: FCO107/108.

CHAPTER 10 – LEADERSHIP CODE

Constitutional Committee

The possible inclusion of a Leadership Code was discussed in a working paper presented to the Committee.[173] The Code which became Chapter 10 was adopted after a short discussion on 11 August 1979.[174]

66. Conduct of leaders

(1) Any person defined as a leader in Article 67 has a duty to conduct himself in such a way, both in his public and private life, so as not to –

    (a) place himself in a position in which he has or could have a conflict of interests or in which the fair exercise of his public or official duties might be compromised;

    (b) demean his office or position;

    (c) allow his integrity to be called into question; or

    (d) endanger or diminish respect for and confidence in the integrity of the Government of the Republic of Vanuatu.

(2) In particular, a leader shall not use his office for personal gain or enter into any transaction or engage in any enterprise or activity that might be expected to give rise to doubt in the public mind as to whether he is carrying out or has carried out the duty imposed by subarticle (1).

Commentary

Any advice of members of the Council of Ministers to the President to exercise the power to dissolve Parliament under Article 28(3) does not involve those members in a contravention of the duty in Article 66(1)(a) to avoid a "position in which he has or could have a conflict of interests": *Barthelemy v President of the Republic of Vanuatu* [2022] VUSC 158 at [34]. The Supreme Court appeared to consider that a course of political conduct aimed at attempting to maintain a majority government would not involve a "conflict of interests" in the relevant sense.

A purported self-pardon under Article 38 by the Acting President amounted to a breach of Article 66(1)(a) because it was a breach of the duty not to place himself in a position of conflict of interest: *Vohor v President of the Republic of Vanuatu* [2015] VUCA 40 at [23]. It also amounted to a breach of Articles 66(1)(b), (c), (d); *Vohor* at [24].

---

[173] Working paper R3: Minutes 255-257. See also the submission by the New Hebrides Council of Churches at Minutes 258-259.

[174] Minutes 109 (PV35[1]).

67. Definition of a leader

For the purposes of this Chapter, a leader means the President of the Republic, the Prime Minister and other Ministers, Members of Parliament, and such public servants, officers of Government agencies and other officers as may be prescribed by law.

68. Parliament to give effect to this Chapter

Parliament shall by law give effect to the principles of this Chapter.

Commentary

Pursuant to Article 68 the Parliament has enacted the Leadership Code [CAP 240].

CHAPTER 11 – EMERGENCY POWERS

Constitutional Committee

The Articles in this Chapter were discussed on 13 September 1979.[175] Although a longer proposal had originally been drafted,[176] discussion focussed on a shorter proposal[177] and, following the preparation of a further draft which took into account comments made in discussion,[178] the Articles were then approved.[179]

69. Emergency regulations

The Council of Ministers may make regulations for dealing with a public emergency whenever –

(a)   the Republic of Vanuatu is at war; or

(b)   the President of the Republic acting on the advice of the Council of Ministers declares a state of emergency by reason of natural calamity or to prevent a threat to or to restore public order.

70. Period of and renewals of state of emergency

(1)   When Parliament is in session a state of emergency declared under Article 69 shall cease to have effect at the end of 1 week unless approved by a resolution of Parliament supported by two-thirds of its members.

(2)   When Parliament is not in session a state of emergency shall cease to have effect at the end of 2 weeks.

(3)   Where a resolution has been passed in accordance with subarticle (1) the state of emergency approved by it shall remain in force for the period authorised by the resolution except that no such resolution may authorise a state of emergency for more than 3 months at one time.

(4)   Parliament may meet whenever it decides during a state of emergency.

(5)   Parliament may not be dissolved under Article 28(2) or 28(3) during a state of emergency. If the life of a Parliament ends in accordance with Article 28(1) during a state of emergency the former members of that Parliament may meet for the purpose only of considering the state of emergency until the new Parliament first meets.

(6)   Parliament may at any time terminate a state of emergency by a resolution supported by an absolute majority of its members.

---

175   Minutes 157,159 (PV47[2]-[4], [31]-[32]).
176   Working paper R5: Minutes 260 (French).
177   Working paper R5(2): Minutes 262.
178   Working paper R5(3): Minutes 263; FCO107/108.
179   Minutes 159 (PV47[31]).

Constitutional Committee

Articles 70(4)-(6) which prevent Parliament being dissolved and increasing its powers during an emergency were introduced as a result of discussions on 13 September 1979.[180]

Commentary

Article 70(6)

The reference to an "absolute majority of its members" means an absolute majority calculated by reference to the members of the Parliament not including those seats which are vacant: *Speaker of Parliament of the Republic of Vanuatu v Weibur* [2023] VUCA 52 at [18]-[20] (a case decided in relation to Article 43(2)).

---

71. Effect of emergency regulations

(1) Subject to subarticle (2) regulations made by the Council of Ministers in accordance with Article 69 shall have effect notwithstanding the provisions of Chapter 2, Part I except that no regulation shall –

    (a) derogate from the right to life and the freedom from inhuman treatment and forced labour; and

    (b) make provision for the detention of a person without trial for more than 1 month unless such person is an enemy alien.

(2) Regulations made by the Council of Ministers in accordance with Article 69 shall be such as are reasonably necessary in the circumstances of the emergency to which they relate and as are justifiable in a democratic society.

Constitutional Committee

The qualifications on the scope of emergency regulations in Article 71(1)(a) and Article 71(2) were introduced (along with what is now Article 72) as a result of concerns that an earlier draft "could lead to too great an infringement on fundamental rights".[181]

---

[180] Minutes at 157 (PV47[3]-[4]). Compare working paper R5(2) Article 2 (Minutes 262-263) with R5(3) Article 2 (Minutes 263; FCO107/108).

[181] Minutes 157 (PV47[3]-[4]).

72. Complaints to Supreme Court concerning emergency regulations

Any citizen aggrieved by reason of regulations made by the Council of Ministers in accordance with Article 69 may complain to the Supreme Court which shall have jurisdiction to determine the validity of all or any of such regulations.

Constitutional Committee

See annotations to Article 71 above.

CHAPTER 12 – LAND

Constitutional Committee

The issue of land was discussed extensively by the Constitutional Committee, on 23 April 1979,[182] 8 August 1979,[183] 22 August 1979,[184] 3 September 1979,[185] 4 September 1979,[186] 5 September 1979,[187] 6 September 1979[188] and 12 September 1979.[189] The contentious nature of the provisions relating to land was reflected in the number of working papers on the issue. Whether or not to make special provision in relation to urban land, where land had been acquired from customary owners, and the extent to which government approval should be required for transactions with non-indigenous persons were particular issues of contention. The provisions in relation to land were finalised at the meeting on 12 September 1979.[190] The provisions adopted by the Committee were a mix of those described in a number of different working papers prepared for the Committee.[191]

---

73. Land belongs to custom owners

All land in the Republic of Vanuatu belongs to the indigenous custom owners and their descendants.

Constitutional Committee

The words "and their descendants" were added at the meeting of the Committee on 3 September 1979.[192] The minutes record that this change was made in the context of a concern to ensure "that children of mixed blood possessing full custom rights to land, would not have those rights denied by the Constitution".[193]

Commentary

Overall effect

The result of articles 73, 74, 75, 79 (1) and 80 was described in *Ratua Development Ltd v Ndai* [2007] VUCA 23 as follows:

---

[182] FCO107/107 (PV9[1]-[2]).
[183] Minutes 98-100 (PV32[17]-[27]).
[184] Minutes 119-121 (PV38[1]-[5], [7]-[27]).
[185] Minutes 122-124 (PV39[5]-[22]).
[186] Minutes 125-129 (PV40[2]-[12], [21]-[39]).
[187] Minutes 130-133 (PV41[2]-[38]).
[188] Minutes 134-136 (PV42[1]-[23]).
[189] Minutes 153-154 (PV46[6]-[18]).
[190] Minutes 154 (PV46[18]).
[191] See the summary at Minutes 154 (PV46[18]).
[192] Minutes 123 (PV39[13]).
[193] Minutes 123 (PV39[10]).

The result of those Articles is that only indigenous citizens and the Government may own land in Vanuatu. There is, however, nothing in the Constitution to prevent land being leased to other persons, indigenous or non-indigenous, citizen or non-citizen or for such leasehold estates to be sold, mortgaged or otherwise dealt with by their proprietors. Indeed, immediately after Independence, Parliament passed the legislation referred to above to enable that to happen and in particular to provide the opportunity for non-indigenous persons who held freehold titles over land before Independence to acquire leasehold titles over that land. However, the only persons who can be lessors are indigenous citizens who are custom owners or the Government.

In *Killet v Niptik* [2012] VUSC 117 at [20] the Supreme Court described the effect of these provisions at Independence as follows:

> At Independence with the return of all non-public lands to the indigenous people of Vanuatu all prior land alienations and titles were extinguished and the lands were returned to their traditional custom owners and their descendants.

In *Tretham Constructions Ltd v Malas* [1996] VUSC 1 at 7 the Supreme Court described the alienation of custom land that was possible under the Constitution:

> The Constitution does not prevent land in Vanuatu from being alienated by means of the land leases. So long as such leases do not confer perpetual ownership of the land upon persons who are not indigenous citizens of Vanuatu. Indeed under leases only the enjoyment of land is alienated, not the perpetual ownership. There is therefore no Constitutional bar to the granting of leases which deprive the custom owners of their enjoyment of their land for definite periods of time, even though it may deprive them and their descendants of such enjoyment for several generations.
>
> …
>
> The indigenous custom owner under the Constitution is entitled to perpetual ownership of his custom land, he has no special Constitutional or other rights to occupation or enjoyment over land that he has leased to others, or that has been leased perfectly legally by the government through the Minister, under the laws of the land.

"land"

The reference to "land" in Articles 73 includes inland waters and territorial seas, including the seabed: *Terra Holdings Ltd v Sope* [2012] VUCA 16 at [35], [40]; *Migale Ltd v Republic of Vanuatu* [2021] VUCA 25 at [27], [29].

---

74. Basis of ownership and use

The rules of custom shall form the basis of ownership and use of land in the Republic of Vanuatu.

Commentary

Proof of custom

Custom is a question of fact not of law: *Lekum v Fresher* [2020] VUSC 257 at 19. It must be applicable to the circumstances of the case, not inconsistent with any written law, justice, morality or good order, and is then applied and enforced by the courts: *Lekum* at [19]. Custom may vary from place to place and hence is dependent upon a finding as to custom in a particular area: *Lekum* at [24]. Custom in relation to land may be different from custom in relation to a chiefly title: *Lekum* at [25].

Disposition of land by will

Article 74 of the Constitution does not permit disposition of customary land, or an interest in custom land, through a will; its disposition is to be determined in accordance with custom: *Estate of Chichirua* [2015] VUSC 122 at [23]. Similarly, custom land is not subject to a statutory disposition upon intestacy: *Chichirua* at [26]-[28].

Status of women

Nothing in articles 73 and 74 denies to women the rights in Article 5(1)(d), (k) to "protection of the law" and "equal treatment under the law" "without discrimination on the grounds of… sex". As a consequence, while custom law must provide the basis for determining ownership and use of land any rule of custom which discriminates against women cannot be applied: *Noel v Tito* [1995] VUSC 3 at 11; *Lapenmal v Awop* [2016] VUSC 90 at [36]-[37]. The contrary was held in *Nathan v Albert* [2004] VUSC 29 at 7 without reference to the earlier decision in *Noel v Tito*.

---

75. Perpetual ownership

Only indigenous citizens of the Republic of Vanuatu who have acquired their land in accordance with a recognised system of land tenure shall have perpetual ownership of their land.

---

76. National land law

Parliament, after consultation with the Malvatumauri Council of Chiefs, shall provide for the implementation of Articles 73, 74 and 75 in a national land law and may make different provision for different categories of land, one of which shall be urban land.

Constitutional Committee

The issue of how to address urban land which was owned by persons other than the customary owners received extensive consideration. Different formulations appeared in a number of working papers.[194] The draft ultimately accepted was drafted by Professor Ghai in order to reach a position that all parties could accept.[195] The making of "different provision for different categories of land one of which shall be urban land" was intended to allow Parliament to make different provision but not tie it down "in matters of detail".[196]

The requirement to consult with the National Council of Chiefs (now the Malvatumauri Council of Chiefs) at the commencement of the Article resulted from a proposal[197] by the French and British Ministers at the Constitutional Conference.[198]

Amendments

The Constitution (Sixth) (Amendment) Act No 27 of 2013 deleted the reference in Article 76 to "National Council of Chiefs"and inserted in its place "Malvatumauri Council of Chiefs".

Commentary

The provisions of Chapter 12 have been implemented by the Land Reform Act [CAP 123].

---

77. Compensation

Parliament shall prescribe such criteria for the assessment of compensation and the manner of its payment as it deems appropriate to persons whose interests are adversely affected by legislation under this Chapter.

---

78. Customary institutions to resolve land ownership and disputes

(1)	Parliament by enactment shall formalise the recognition of appropriate customary institutions or procedures to resolve land ownership or any disputes over custom land.

(2)	Parliament may recognise an institution as a customary institution by enactment for the purposes of subarticle (1).

(3)	Despite the provisions of Chapter 8 of the Constitution, the final substantive decisions reached by customary institutions or procedures in accordance with Article 74, after being recorded in writing, are binding

---

[194]	Working papers J1(3) Article 7 (Minutes 248 (French)), J4 Article 7 (Minutes 250 (French)), J4(2) (Minutes 251), J4(4) (FCO107/108), J4(5) (FCO107/108).
[195]	Minutes 154 (PV46[14]-[18]).
[196]	Minutes 154 (PV46[14]).
[197]	Working paper J4(6): FCO107/109.
[198]	Minutes at 177 (PV51[2]).

> in law and are not subject to appeal or any other form of review by any Court of law.
>
> (4) Subarticle (3) does not apply to any matter being referred to a Court before the commencement of this amendment.
>
> (5) Where consequent to the provisions of this Chapter there is a dispute concerning the custom ownership of land the government may hold such land and manage it in the interests of disputing parties until the dispute is resolved.

Amendments

Article 78 was originally Article 76. As originally made it provided:

> 76. (1) Where consequent on the provisions of this Chapter, there is a dispute concerning the ownership of alienated land the Government shall hold such land until the dispute is resolved.
>
> (2) The Government shall arrange for the appropriate customary institutions or procedures to resolve disputes concerning the ownership of custom land.

The Constitution (Sixth) (Amendment) Act No 27 of 2013 repealed the article and substituted it in its present form.

Commentary

Original version of Article 78

In *Valele Family v Touru* [2002] VUCA 3 at 8 the Court of Appeal said, in relation to the original version of Article 78:

> Article 78 must be read as a whole, and in light of all the other provisions of the Constitution. In particular, Article 78(2) must be read subject to Article 78(1). Article 78(1) expressly limits the operation of Article 78 to disputes concerning the ownership of alienated land. In such a case the land is held by the Government until the dispute is resolved, and Article 78 (2) spells out what the Government is to do whilst it holds the land. The Government must arrange to have the dispute resolved by 'the appropriate customary institution or procedures'.

It went on to find (at 9): "Article 78(2) should be interpreted as meaning institutions and procedures established within the constitutional court system." So far as disputes outside the scope of Article 78 were concerned, the Court held (at 9) that they were required to be dealt with by the courts.

The provisions of the Island Courts Act [CAP 167] and the inclusion of assessors knowledgeable in custom to sit with a Supreme Court judge on an appeal met the requirement of Article 78(2) in its original form: *Matarave v Talivo* [2010] VUCA 3 at 8.

Effect of amendments

The effect of the amendments made by the Constitution (Sixth) (Amendment) Act No 27 of 2013 was described in *Tura v Taftumol Family* [2024] VUCA 20 at [13]-[14]:

> 13. Before the Sixth Amendment under these provisions the determination of legal rights was vested in one or other of the two court systems. The Island Courts had the exclusive jurisdiction to resolve disputes concerning ownership of custom land subject only to a limited right of appeal to the Supreme Court thereby establishing the rights and obligations of the parties in relation to ownership and interests in the land. The rights of the parties in all matters apart from custom land ownership and the enforcement of those rights fell to be determined under the general jurisdiction of the Supreme Court and the application of the laws of the Republic.
>
> 14. By the Sixth Amendment, Article 51 was altered to exclude the power of Parliament to make provision for the manner of ascertainment of the relevant rules of custom relating to the ownership of custom land, and Article 78 was altered to require Parliament to formalise the recognition of appropriate customary institutions or procedures to resolve land ownership or any dispute over custom land. These alterations led to the enactment of the [Custom Land Management Act 2013] which was assented to on 16 January 2014. The CLMA enacted an entirely new legal system for the resolution of disputes relating to custom land ownership and thereby the establishment of the rights and obligations of parties to the dispute, including as to the rights and obligations of holders of secondary rights. Subject only to the transitional provisions, the CLMA entirely replaced the determinative role previously exercised by the Island Court. The Sixth Amendment did not alter Article 75 of the Constitution.

The Supreme Court has limited supervisory powers in relation to an Island Court (Land) under s 47 of the Custom Land Management Act No 33 of 2013 which allows applications to the Supreme Court in certain limited circumstances but not appeals from the Island Court (Land): *Kalmet v Kalmermer* [2024] VUCA 46 at [16]-[17].

Article 78(3)

In *Kallon v Mera* [2024] VUCA 1, Mera had claims to be custom owner of certain areas of land. As a result of inadequate notice, those claims had not been considered or determined by the Nakamal and other claims to the same land were heard and determined. Because the Mera claims had not been considered or determined by the Nakamal, Article 78(3) did not preclude proceedings in the Supreme Court. At [32] the Court of Appeal said:

> Neither decision could be said to be a "final substantive decision" because the claimant's claim was not heard and no decision on its merits was made in respect of it. A "substantive" decision is a decision made on the merits of a claim or dispute. A "final substantive decision" is a decision that decides a claim on its merits after a procedurally fair process has been followed. In this case, a procedurally fair process was not followed because Mr Mera was not given

adequate, or any, notice of the hearing to determine custom ownership, resulting in his claim not being heard and decided on its merits.

---

79. Land transactions

(1)　Notwithstanding Articles 73, 74 and 75 land transactions between an indigenous citizen and either a non-indigenous citizen or a non-citizen shall only be permitted with the consent of the Government.

(2)　The consent required under subarticle (1) shall be given unless the transaction is prejudicial to the interests of –

　　(a)　the custom owner or owners of the land;

　　(b)　the indigenous citizen where he is not the custom owner;

　　(c)　the community in whose locality the land is situated; or

　　(d)　the Republic of Vanuatu.

Constitutional Committee

At the meeting on 6 September 1979[199] the Committee agreed to a draft of the clause which became Article 79 as follows:

> Notwithstanding articles 1, 2 and 3, the Government shall be consulted on any land dealings between indigenous citizens on the one hand and non-indigenous citizens or foreigners on the other hand, and that Government authorization shall be given unless any such transaction is prejudicial to the interests of the customary owner or owners of the land, the indigenous citizen, the local community or the nation.

The following sentence that had been included at the end of this clause was deleted: "Any party specified in this article may seek the ruling of the Supreme Court for its rights under this article."

---

80. Government may own land

Notwithstanding Articles 73 and 74 the Government may own land acquired by it in the public interest.

Constitutional Committee

This clause was agreed to by the Committee on 6 September 1979[200]

---

[199]　Minutes 135 (PV42[18]-[20]).
[200]　Minutes 135 (PV42[20]) accepting Article 5 of working paper J2 (Minutes 249).

Commentary

Once land becomes public land, custom owners cease to have rights of ownership although they may have rights to compensation under Article 77: *Kalomtak Wiwi Family v Minister of Lands* [2004] VUSC 47 at 6.

---

81. Redistribution of land

(1) Notwithstanding Articles 73 and 74 the Government may buy land from custom owners for the purpose of transferring ownership of it to indigenous citizens or indigenous communities from over-populated islands.

(2) When redistributing land in accordance with subarticle (1), the Government shall give priority to ethnic, linguistic, customary and geographical ties.

Constitutional Committee

This article was agreed to by the Committee on 6 September 1979.[201]

---

[201] Minutes 135 (PV42[20]) accepting Article 7 of working paper J2 (Minutes 249-250).

CHAPTER 13 – DECENTRALISATION

82. Legislation for decentralisation

The Republic of Vanuatu, conscious of the importance of decentralisation to enable the people fully to participate in the government of their Provincial Government Region, shall enact legislation necessary to realize that ideal.

Constitutional Committee

The issue of decentralisation was one of the most contentious issues in the deliberations of the Constitutional Committee. While there was strong support for decentralisation there were significant differences and debate as to how it should be implemented.[202] The matter was discussed at length at multiple meetings of the Committee (10 April 1979,[203] 19 June 1979,[204] 3 August 1979,[205] 6 August 1979,[206] 10 August 1979,[207] 20-21 August 1979[208] and 15 September 1979[209]). The final form of the Chapter reflects a revised proposal circulated as part of a collection of revisions proposed by the French and British Ministers at the Constitutional Conference on 18 September 1979.[210] The final form of the provisions was in more general terms than provided for in earlier drafts[211] and incorporated a requirement that legislation relating to the powers and administration of regions be passed by a two thirds majority of the Parliament. As a result of the proposals made by the French and British Ministers at the Constitutional Conference, specific provision was also made in Article 94 for the establishment of Regional Councils in Tanna and Santo based on elections held following the Exchange of Notes but prior to Independence.

The Articles adopted at the Constitutional Conference were replaced as a result of the Constitution First Amendment Act No 10 of 1980: see annotations to Article 83 below.

Amendments

The Constitution (Sixth) (Amendment) Act No 27 of 2013 removed the reference to "Local Government Regions" and substituted "Provincial Government Regions".

---

202 Minutes 107 (PV34[14]).
203 Minutes 32 (PV8)[11]-[14]).
204 Minutes 38-39 (PV12[1]-[8]).
205 Minutes 87-89 (PV29[13]-[28]).
206 Minutes 91-93 (PV30[14]-[23]).
207 Minutes 106-108 (PV34[1]-[24]).
208 Minutes 113-116(PV36[2]-[28]), 117-118 (PV37[2]-[12]).
209 Minutes 166-171 (PV49[20]-[69]).
210 Working paper A9(4) is in FCO107/109.
211 The form of the Articles going into the Constitutional Conference is in working paper A9(3): Minutes at 206-207; FCO107/108.

---

83. Provincial Government Councils

The legislation shall provide for the division of the Republic of Vanuatu into Provincial Government Regions and for each region to be administered by a Provincial Government Council on which shall be representatives of custom chiefs.

Constitutional Committee

See annotations to Article 82 above.

Amendments

Article 83 (then Article 81) originally provided:

> 81. (1) Each region may elect a regional Council in accordance with a law which shall in particular provide for the representation of custom chiefs within such Council.
>
> (2) As soon as a regional Council is elected, it shall start negotiations with the Government in order to prepare proposals for legislation providing for the powers and administration of the region.
>
> (3) The proposals for legislation referred to in paragraph (2) shall be submitted to Parliament which shall adopt them by the votes of at least two-thirds of the members of Parliament.

The Constitution First Amendment Act No 10 of 1980 substituted the original terms of Article 83 (then Article 81) so as to put it largely in its current form, although it referred to "Local Government Regions" and a "Local Government Council". The same Act made amendments elsewhere in the Constitution to change the references to regions and regional councils to local government regions and local government councils. The Act also revoked Article 94 which related to "Regional Councils before Independence" which were to be elected following the Exchange of Notes but prior to Independence.

The Constitution (Sixth) (Amendment) Act No 27 of 2013 removed the references to "Local Government Councils" and "Local Government Regions" and substituted "Provincial Government Councils" and "Provincial Government Regions".

CHAPTER 14 – AMENDMENT OF THE CONSTITUTION

84. Bills for amendment of Constitution

A bill for an amendment of the Constitution may be introduced either by the Prime Minister or any other member of Parliament.

---

85. Procedure for passing Constitutional amendments

A bill for an amendment of the Constitution shall not come into effect unless it is supported by the votes of no less than two-thirds of all the members of Parliament at a special sitting of Parliament at which three-quarters of the members are present. If there is no such quorum at the first sitting, Parliament may meet and make a decision by the same majority a week later even if only two-thirds of the members are present.

Constitutional Committee

Amendment of the Constitution was dealt with on 6 August 1979,[212] 11 August 1979,[213] 12 September 1979[214] and 13 September 1979.[215] On 12 September 1979 the Committee discussed the matters in relation to which an amendment required a referendum and the majority required in Parliament for an amendment to be adopted. Two alternatives were proposed: a two thirds majority with a quorum of three quarters but with a minimum requirement that the proposal be approved by a majority of the total membership of Parliament; a two thirds majority of the total members of Parliament. A revised proposal was put forward on 13 September 1979 which corresponds to the terms of Article 85.[216] On 13 September 1979 the Articles were approved and it was agreed that they should form a separate chapter of the Constitution.[217]

Commentary

A proposed amendment to the Constitution which would insert a provision which is ambiguous is not unconstitutional: *President of the Republic of Vanuatu v Speaker of Parliament* [2025] VUSC 286 at [49]. Instead it triggers a process where courts try to interpret the law to be constitutional.

---

[212] Minutes 91 (PV30[11]-[14]).

[213] Minutes 111-112 (PV35[26]-[36]).

[214] Minutes 154-156 (PV46[19]-[31]).

[215] Minutes 157-158 (PV47[1], [12]-[14]).

[216] Minutes 158 (PV47[1], [12]), Working paper F1(2) (Minutes 235; FCO107/108).

[217] Minutes 158 (PV47[14]).

> ## 86. Amendments requiring support of referendums
>
> A bill for an amendment of a provision of the Constitution regarding the status of Bislama, English and French, the electoral system, or the parliamentary system, passed by Parliament under Article 85, shall not come into effect unless it has been supported in a national referendum.

Constitutional Committee

Both working papers presented to the Committee included a requirement for a referendum to approve certain changes to the Constitution.[218] The requirements for a referendum were discussed by the Committee on 12 September 1979.[219]

Amendment

What is now Article 86 (previously Article 84) originally included amongst the matters which would require approval by referendum: "the powers and organisation of Regional Councils". This requirement was deleted by the Constitution First Amendment Act No 10 of 1980.

Commentary

Article 86 requires that the bill shall not come into effect unless it has been supported by a national referendum. It is therefore not essential that the Speaker certify, as required by s 13 of the Acts of Parliament Act, that the bill was passed with the support of a national referendum prior to providing it to the President if the bill itself provides that it does not come into effect unless it is supported by a national referendum: *Kalsakau v Republic of Vanuatu* [2024] VUSC 81 at [49].

A challenge to the constitutional validity of the Constitution (Eighth) (Amendment) Act No 21 of 2023 that was brought prior to the conduct of the referendum on 29 May 2024 was dismissed as premature in *Kalsakau v Republic of Vanuatu* [2024] VUCA 31 as at that time it did not affect the rights of any person and there could be no breach of any rights under Article 5(1) of the Constitution.

"parliamentary system"

In *Vohor v Attorney-General* [2004] VUCA 22 at 18 the Court of Appeal said "… the Parliamentary system was one adopted by the Republic of Vanuatu on Independence Day and that system must include all the processes of electing Members of Parliament right up to the appointment of government ministers…" It rejected a submission that, having regard to what was said during the deliberations of the Constitutional Committee in 1979, the reference to the "Parliamentary system" in Article 86 should be confined to whether there was a Parliamentary system or a presidential system.

---

[218] Working paper F1 (FCO107/107), F1(2) (Minutes 235; FCO107/108).
[219] Minutes 155-156 (PV46[20]-[31]).

In *Saemon v Tallis* [2019] VUCA 44, a case arising from a referral under Article 16(4), the Supreme Court and then the Court of Appeal held that the Constitution (Seventh) (Amendment) Act No 1 of 2019 was inconsistent with Article 86 because it made amendments "regarding the Parliamentary system" within the meaning of Article 86 but no national referendum had occurred. The proposed amendments would have allowed for the appointment of Parliamentary Secretaries to whom the Prime Minister could assign responsibility for the conduct of government. A national referendum was required because the amendment would spread responsibility for the conduct of government more widely than the Ministers assigned responsibilities by the Prime Minister pursuant to Article 42 (2) and it increased the proportion of Members of Parliament with responsibility for the conduct of government beyond the limit on the number of Ministers set in Article 40(2).

CHAPTER 15 – TRANSITIONAL PROVISIONS

Constitutional Committee

The working paper[220] which gave rise to what are now Articles 87 – 95 was presented and discussed at the meeting of the Committee on 14 September 1979.[221] Each Article was discussed and all except for what is now Article 92 were approved. Article 92 was approved with an amendment the next day. What was originally Article 94 (deleted shortly after Independence) arose from a proposal by the French and British Ministers at the Constitutional Conference on 18 September 1979.[222]

---

87. First President of the Republic

Notwithstanding Chapter 6 the first President of the Republic shall –

(a) be such person as shall have been elected prior to the Day of Independence by an electoral college constituted for that purpose by the Representative Assembly sitting with the Presidents of the Regional Councils if then established;

(b) assume office on the Day of Independence and hold office in accordance with the provisions of the Constitution.

Constitutional Committee

This Article as set out in a working paper[223] was approved as by the Committee on 14 September 1979.[224]

---

88. First Prime Minister and other Ministers

The persons who immediately before the Day of Independence hold office as Chief Minister or any other Minister shall as from that day hold office as Prime Minister or other Minister, as the case may be, as if they had been elected or appointed thereto under Chapter 7.

Constitutional Committee

This Article, as set out in a working paper,[225] was approved by the Committee on 14 September 1979.[226]

---

[220] Working paper R7: Minutes 265 (French); FCO107/108.
[221] Minutes at 160-163 (PV48).
[222] See Article 94 below.
[223] Working paper R7, Article 1: Minutes 265 (French); FCO107/108.
[224] Minutes at 160 (PV48[7]).
[225] Working paper R7, Article 1: Minutes 265 (French); FCO107/108.
[226] Minutes 162 (PV48[22]).

89. First Parliament

(1) The persons who immediately before the Day of Independence are members of the Representative Assembly shall on that day become members of Parliament and shall hold their seats in Parliament in accordance with the Constitution.

(2) The person who immediately before the Day of Independence holds the office of Chairman of the Representative Assembly shall as from that day act in the office of Speaker of Parliament until a person is elected to hold that office.

(3) The standing orders of the Representative Assembly in force immediately before the Day of Independence shall have effect as from that day as the standing orders of Parliament until modified or replaced under Article 21(5) but shall be construed with such adaptations as may be necessary to bring them into conformity with the Constitution.

(4) Parliament shall, unless sooner dissolved, stand dissolved on the 14 November 1983.

Constitutional Committee

This Article as set out in a working paper[227] was approved by the Committee on 14 September 1979.[228]

90. Existing offices

(1) Subject to the other provisions of the Constitution, a person who immediately before the Day of Independence holds or acts in an office in the service of the Government of the Republic of Vanuatu shall, as from that day, hold or act in that office or the corresponding office established by or under the Constitution on the same terms and conditions as those on which he holds or acts in the office immediately before that day.

(2) Subarticle (1) is without prejudice to the power of Parliament to provide for the compulsory retirement of non-citizen officers to promote localisation of offices.

(3) Notwithstanding Article 57(2), until a citizen of Vanuatu is qualified for appointment to a public office a non-citizen may be appointed to that office but, except in the case of a judge of the Supreme Court, shall be appointed for a limited period.

---

[227] Working paper R7, Article 1: Minutes 265 (French); FCO107/108.
[228] Minutes 162 (PV48[22]).

Constitutional Committee

What became Article 90(2) was inserted at Professor Ghai's suggestion on 14 September 1979 "to help promote the localisation of public offices".[229]

Article 90(3) was added on 15 September 1979.[230]

---

91. Judges of the Supreme Court

Notwithstanding Chapter 8, any person who immediately before the Day of Independence holds office as a judge of the pre-Independence Supreme Court or of a District Court shall as from that day act in the office of judge of the Supreme Court until a substantive appointment is made to that office in accordance with Chapter 8. The President of the Republic may appoint one of them to act as Chief Justice until a substantive appointment is made to that office.

Constitutional Committee

The first sentence of Article 91[231] was approved by the Committee on 14 September 1979.[232] Following the Constitutional Conference the last sentence was added.[233]

---

92. Rights, liabilities and obligations

(1) All rights, liabilities and obligations of the Government of the New Hebrides, whether arising out of contract or otherwise, shall, as from the Day of Independence, be rights, liabilities and obligations of the Republic of Vanuatu.

(2) Nothing in subarticle (1) shall prevent the Government of the Republic of Vanuatu renegotiating rights, liabilities or obligations assumed under that subarticle.

Constitutional Committee

What is now Article 92(1) was considered by the Committee on 14 September 1979.[234] Concern was expressed as to the uncertainty as to precisely what rights, liabilities and obligations would be inherited, having regard to the fact that some contracts would have been made by Resident Commissioners on behalf of their respective national services as distinct from the Condominium Administration or the pre-Independence New Hebrides Government. The issue was revisited

---

229 Minutes 160 (PV48[3]). It was approved at Minutes 162 (PV48[22]).
230 Minutes 164 (PV49[6]). Working paper R7(2) (FCO107/108) also resulted in the amendment of Article 57(2).
231 Working paper R7, Article 1: Minutes 265 (French); FCO107/108
232 Minutes 162 (PV48[22]).
233 See amendment titled "Chapter 15 Transitional" in FCO107/109.
234 Minutes 162 (PV48[23]-[27]).

the next day[235] and Professor Ghai proposed what is now Article 92(2). He said that it seemed the liabilities would be those of the pre-Independence government and not of the Resident Commissioners and that the Article did not deal with international treaties made between the New Hebrides and foreign governments.

---

93. Electoral system

After the general elections next following the Exchange of Notes providing for the entry into force of this Article, the Representative Assembly shall set up a Committee with equal representation of all political groups to make recommendations on an electoral system based on Article 17(1).

The recommendations of the Committee shall be included in a law enacted by Parliament by a two-thirds majority of its members at a special sitting of Parliament when at least three-fourths of the members are present. If there is no such quorum at the first sitting, Parliament may meet and make a decision by the same majority a week later even if only two-thirds of the members are present.

Constitutional Committee

What is now Article 93[236] was approved by the Committee on 14 September 1979.[237]

Commentary

In *Kalpokas v Hakwa* [2002] VUCA 12 at 4-5 it was argued that the Representation of the People Act [CAP 146] was given "special constitutional status" by reason of Article 93 because it was the outcome of the process set out in Article 93. The Court of Appeal identified the factual matters that would be required in order to establish this proposition and said that no evidence had been provided in that case to establish those matters.

---

94. Legal proceedings

All legal proceedings, whether civil or criminal, pending immediately before the Day of Independence before any court in Vanuatu shall be disposed of on and after that day in accordance with general or specific directions given by the Supreme Court subject to any law which may be enacted for that purpose.

Constitutional Committee

Article 94[238] was approved by the Committee on 14 September 1979.[239]

---

[235] Minutes 164 (PV49[2]-[5]).
[236] Working paper R7, Article 7: Minutes 265 (French); FCO107/108.
[237] Minutes 162 (PV48[28]).
[238] Working paper R7, Article 8: Minutes at 265 (French), FCO107/108.
[239] Minutes 162 (PV48[30]).

Amendments

Article 94 was originally Article 92. For commentary on the article that was originally Article 94, see "Original Article 94 (deleted)" after the commentary on Article 95 below.

95. Existing law

(1)   Until otherwise provided by Parliament, all Joint Regulations and subsidiary legislation made thereunder in force immediately before the Day of Independence shall continue in operation on and after that day as if they had been made in pursuance of the Constitution and shall be construed with such adaptations as may be necessary to bring them into conformity with the Constitution.

(2)   Until otherwise provided by Parliament, the British and French laws in force or applied in Vanuatu immediately before the Day of Independence shall on and after that day continue to apply to the extent that they are not expressly revoked or incompatible with the independent status of Vanuatu and wherever possible taking due account of custom.

(3)   Customary law shall continue to have effect as part of the law of the Republic of Vanuatu.

Constitutional Committee

At the meeting of the Committee on 14 September 1979 Professor Ghai proposed amendments to the drafting of what is now Article 95 in the relevant working paper.[240] He proposed deleting paragraphs at the end of the article addressing the application of laws to corporate bodies and a requirement that the laws apply "to the extent required to ensure that substantial justice obtains" and instead:

(a)   adding at the end of what is now Article 95(2) the words "and wherever possible taking due account of custom";

(b)   adding what is now Article 95(3) in relation to customary law.

Professor Ghai explained the addition of paragraph (3) was "intended to keep in effect those Joint Regulations that provided for the application of customary law".[241] There was some discussion of this paragraph but the Article was approved as amended by Professor Ghai. [242]

---

[240] Working paper R7: Minutes 265 (French); FCO107/108.
[241] Minutes 163 (PV48[31]).
[242] Minutes 163 (PV48[36]).

Commentary

Article 95(1)

Article 95(1) is concerned with the continuation of "Joint Regulations and subsidiary legislation made thereunder". That is a reference to joint regulations made under Articles 7 and 8 of the Anglo-French Protocol of 1914: see the commentary on "Pre-independence laws" below.

Those laws are continued in force "as if they had been made in pursuance of the Constitution". In *Banga v Waiwo* [1996] VUSC 5 at 6 the Supreme Court held that:

(a)   laws continued under Article 95(1) and Article 95(2) became the law of Vanuatu and applied to "everyone in Vanuatu equally";

(b)   the application of different laws to British subjects, French subjects, optants and native new Hebrideans was not something which was continued after Independence or compatible with the independent status of the Republic;

(c)   it was the intention of the Constitution that all laws applicable in the New Hebrides prior to the Day of Independence should apply to all people.

Article 95(2)

Article 95(2) is concerned with the continuation of "the British and French laws in force or applied in Vanuatu". These were laws other than Joint Regulations. They included British or French laws that applied to British or French subjects and, in the case of British subjects, the common law: see the commentary on "Pre-independence laws" below. These laws continue to apply "to the extent that they are not expressly revoked or incompatible with the independent status of Vanuatu".

The reference to "British" laws should be understood as laws of the United Kingdom.[243] The reference to "British" laws may have been used because the Anglo French Protocol of 1914 was between the British and French Governments.

The operation of Article 95(2) was considered in *Banga v Waiwo* [1996] VUSC 5 at 6: see the commentary on Article 95(1) above. As to the application of British and French law equally to all in Vanuatu irrespective of nationality, see also *Selb Pacific Ltd v Mouton* [1996] VUSC 4 at 2.

Laws continued by Article 95(2) apply to persons whether or not they were resident in Vanuatu prior to Independence: *Clements v Hong Kong and Shanghai Banking Corporation* [1988] VULawRp 5; [1980-1994] Van LR 416.

---

[243] See n 2 above.

In *Harrisen v Holloway (No 1)* [1984] VULawRp 13; [1980-1994] Van LR 106 at 1 the Supreme Court found that the Police Act 1964 (UK) was incompatible with the independent status of Vanuatu and hence could not be applied.

Article 95(2): "otherwise provided"

In *Joli v Joli* [2003] VUCA 27 the Court of Appeal considered whether the terms of the Matrimonial Causes Act [CAP 192] "otherwise provided" so as to render the Matrimonial Causes Act 1973 (UK) no longer applicable. The Vanuatu Act covered some but not all of the same subject matters as the British Act. The Court concluded that the Vanuatu Act did not evidence an intention "to completely cover the field" in relation to ancillary matters following the dissolution of a marriage. As a consequence, the British Act still had a residual operation pursuant to Article 95(2) allowing adjustment of property interests. The Court (at 9) gave some consideration as to how custom could be taken into account under the continued provisions of the British Act.

Article 95(2): conflicting laws

Under Article 95(2) the British and French laws in force immediately prior to independence that were in effect became laws of Vanuatu following independence. Following independence there is a single body of Vanuatu law even if it derives from different pre-independence sources, and that law may overlap or be in conflict: *In re MM* [2014] VUSC 78 at [26], [29]-[31]. Where Parliament has not otherwise provided and there are both British and French laws that can apply, there is no right of election between them: *Banga v Waivo* [1996] VUSC 5 at 9.

Where the laws are in conflict, there is no statutory authority to guide a court as to how that conflict should be resolved: *In re MM* at [36]. The invocation of "substantial justice" as a means of resolving conflicts articulated in *Banga v Waiwo* [1996] VUSC 5 at 9 (and adopted in *Montgolfier v Gaillande* [2013] VUSC 39) was doubted in *In re MM* [2014] VUSC 78 at [33]-[36].

As a consequence, where a pre-independence French law permitted an adoption but a pre-independence British law prohibited the adoption, in the absence of any Vanuatu statute, the law of Vanuatu established by Article 95(2) prohibited the adoption: *In re MM* at [40].

In *Pentecost Pacific Ltd v Hnaloane* [1984] VUCA 4, a case where the substantive law applicable was a statute of Vanuatu, the Court of Appeal said, in relation to the procedural law to be applied, "the choice between French law and English law will be decided according to the nationality of the defendant".

Article 95(2): "taking due account of custom"

The relationship between pre-Independence laws applied as part of the post-Independence law of Vanuatu and custom is not made clear by the text of Article 95(2). In *In re MM* [2014] VUSC 78 at [49] the Supreme Court explained that the qualification ("taking due account of custom") may or may not (depending on the circumstances) affect the outcome of the application of a pre-Independence law. In that case, in order to inform the court about custom, evidence was obtained from the President of the Malvatumauri Council of Chiefs. The Council was described (at [51]) as "the authorised repository of knowledge and advice on all matters of custom, tradition and cultural matters in Vanuatu".

Article 95(3)

When considering British and French law applying at Independence it is possible, to a certain extent, to take into account subsequent developments in British or French case law. In *Zuchetto v Republic of Vanuatu* [2014] VUCA 17 at [15] the Court of Appeal said:

> While the Constitution makes no reference to developments in the British or French law since independence, this Court can derive assistance from cases after independence that are consistent with the pre-Independence law and consider it further.

Article 95(3) customary law

Article 95(3) operates in the context of Article 47(1) which limits the role of customary law in the administration of justice. It cannot have effect if inconsistent with the Constitution or laws made by the Parliament. Where a person has offended against the criminal laws enacted by the Parliament, customary law does not affect a person's criminal liability: *Viraleo v Loloi* [2022] VUCA 33 at [12]. Nor can it effect a person's civil liability: *Loloi v Leo* [2021] VUSC 289 at [21]-[25].

Custom is a question of fact not of law: *Lekum v Fresher* [2020] VUSC 257 at 19. It must be applicable to the circumstances of the case, not inconsistent with any written law, justice, morality or good order, and is then applied and enforced by the courts: *Lekum* at [19]. Custom may vary from place to place and hence is dependent upon a finding as to custom in a particular area: *Lekum* at [24]. Custom in relation to land may be different from custom in relation to a chiefly title: *Lekum* at [25].

Pre-Independence laws

The laws applicable in the New Hebrides from the coming into force of the Anglo French Protocol of 1914 in 1922 up until Independence and the application of those laws to British subjects, French subjects, optants and native New Hebrideans is described in *Banga v Waiwo* [1996] VUSC 5 at 4-5. In *Joli v Joli* [2003] VUCA 27 at 4 the Court of Appeal described the law immediately before and after Independence as follows:

> Immediately before the Day of Independence on 30 July 1980, laws which applied in Vanuatu included statutes of general application in force in England on 1st January 1976 as well as the principles of the English common law and equity: see the High Court of the New Hebrides Regulations 1976. Under the terms of

the Anglo French Protocol of 1914, those laws would not have applied to French citizens and "optants" to the French legal system. Their rights were governed by French law under the parallel legal system then in force. At Independence, laws in force immediately beforehand were continued in operation by Article 95 of the Constitution …

The effect of Article 95 was to make the law in force immediately after independence, whether derived from French law or English law or otherwise, law of general application to everyone within the Republic equally without distinction based on nationality or ethnic origin.

Pursuant to the High Court of New Hebrides Regulations 1976 "all United Kingdom statutes of general application in force in England on 1 January 1976" were declared applicable to the Condominium "so far as circumstances admit": *Ayamiseba v Government of the Republic of Vanuatu* [2008] VUSC 15 at [14].

The civil procedure rules in force at independence were the Western Pacific High Court (Civil Procedure) Rules 1964 which were continued in force after independence by Article 95(2) (until they were replaced in 2003): *Inter-Pacific Investments Ltd v Sulis* [2007] VUSC 21 at [10].

The Crown Proceedings Act 1947 (UK) applied in Vanuatu at the date of Independence. It was not incompatible with the independent status of Vanuatu and although it made reference to "the Crown", that is simply an expression which embodies the state or government. It therefore became part of the law of Vanuatu even though there are some aspects which were inappropriate for Vanuatu which will not need to be applied: *Ayamiseba v Government of the Republic of Vanuatu* [2008] VUSC 15 at [15]-[16].

Laws permitting the award of interest on judgments were continued pursuant to Article 95(2): *Naylor v Foundas* [2004] VUCA 26 at 4.

Pre independence court judgments

The Anglo French Protocol of 1914 established a joint administration for the New Hebrides by the French and British Governments. Decisions made by the Joint Courts and by other courts established under the protocol have continuing force and effect after independence: *Colardeau v Mammelin* [1980] VULawRp 1; [1980-1994] Van LR 1; *Kalotiti v Kaltapang* [2007] VUCA 25 at 4-5.

The common law

Where no specific legislation has been passed in Vanuatu dealing with a particular topic since Independence, the fallback position, as necessitated by Article 95(2) of the Constitution of Vanuatu, is that the common law as to that topic in the Republic of Vanuatu relies on both received British and French law as at 29 July 1980: *Russet v Huang* [2022] VUSC 244 at [30].

Equitable principles relevant to the determination of the property disputes between de facto couples continue under Article 95(2): *Mariango v Nalau* [2007] VUCA 15 at [18].

Judicial review

In *Vohor v President of the Republic of Vanuatu* [2015] VUCA 40 at [28] the Court of Appeal said:

> The power to grant judicial review in Vanuatu arises from the continuation of British and French law that applied on independence under Article 95(2) of the Constitution, and is expressly recognised in rule 17.4 of the [Civil Procedure] Rules. Rule 17.4(1)(a) and (b) provide for the making of a declaratory order, a mandatory order, a prohibiting order, and a quashing order, about a decision.
>
> The jurisdiction arises from the position of the Supreme Court having, as it has been put in the United Kingdom in relation to that country, "a constitutional role… as the guardian of standards of legality (R (Cart) v Upper Tribunal [2011] QB 120 at [35]).

Original Article 94 (deleted)

Amendment

The article originally numbered 94 related to the establishment of Regional Councils on Tanna and Santo following the Exchange of Notes on 23 October 1979 but prior to Independence. It was deleted by the Constitution First Amendment Act No 10 of 1980.

Commentary

The article originally numbered 94 arose from a proposal[244] by the French and British Ministers at the Constitutional Conference.[245] It provided for the election of Regional Councils on Tanna and Santo and for those Councils to negotiate with the government in order to prepare proposals for legislation for decentralisation for Tanna and Santo before Independence. The proposal was agreed to at the Constitutional Conference but Article 94 was deleted shortly after Independence.

---

[244] Working paper R7(4): FCO107/109.
[245] Minutes 177 (PV51[2]).

SCHEDULE 1

ELECTION OF THE PRESIDENT OF THE REPUBLIC

(Article 34)

1. The election of the President of the Republic shall take place within 3 weeks of the end of the term of office of the previous President.

2.(1) The electoral college may proceed to elect the President of the Republic at its first meeting if at least three-fourths of its member are present.

   (2) If there is no such quorum, the electoral college shall meet again 48 hours later and may lawfully proceed to elect the President if at least two-thirds of its members are present.

3. The candidate who obtains the support of two-thirds of the members of the electoral college shall be elected President of the Republic.

Constitutional Committee

The terms of Schedule 1 arose from amendments proposed by the French and British Ministers and adopted at the Constitutional Conference on 18 September 1979.[246] The previous draft of the schedule contained an initial requirement that the candidate obtain the support of two thirds of the members voting but then permitted the exclusion of the candidate with the lowest number of votes and ultimately, on a third ballot the election of the candidate with the highest number of votes.[247]

Commentary

Schedule 1 does not address what occurs in a circumstance where no candidate obtains a two thirds majority. It assumes that some compromise will be reached to allow that threshold to be passed.

---

[246] Working paper C7(9): FCO107/109 proposed by the Ministers at Minutes 177 (PV51[2]).

[247] Working paper C7: FCO107/108.

SCHEDULE 2

ELECTION OF THE PRIME MINISTER

(Article 41)

1. The candidate who obtains the support of an absolute majority of the members of Parliament shall be elected Prime Minister.

2. If no candidate is elected under paragraph 1, a second ballot shall be taken but the candidate obtaining the lowest number of votes in the first ballot shall be eliminated.

3. If on the second ballot no candidate obtains the support specified in paragraph 1, further ballots shall be held, each time eliminating the candidate with the lowest vote in the preceding ballot until one candidate receives the support specified in paragraph 1, or if only two candidates remain the support of a simple majority.

Constitutional Committee

The working paper upon which Schedule 2 is based[248] had clause 3 concluding "or if the number of candidates is reduced to two, the candidate with the higher vote". At some point (probably immediately prior to the Constitutional Conference) a drafting change was made so that it now reads "or if only two candidates remain the support of a simple majority".

Commentary

The reference to an "an absolute majority of the members of Parliament" in clause 1 of Schedule 2 means an absolute majority calculated by reference to the members of the Parliament not including those seats which are vacant: *Speaker of Parliament of the Republic of Vanuatu v Weibur* [2023] VUCA 52 at [18]-[20] (a case decided in relation to Article 43(2)).

Even where there is only one candidate, a secret ballot in which the candidate obtains the support of the absolute majority of Members of Parliament is mandatory: *Kilman v Natapei* [2011] VUCA 24 at [8]-[9].

---

[248] Working paper C7: FCO107/108.

Table of working papers of the Constitutional Committee

Working papers of the Constitutional Committee are identified by their page number in the Minutes or their location in the Foreign and Commonwealth Office files obtained from the National Archives of the United Kingdom: see the explanation of sources ("Sources of extrinsic materials") at page 4 above. Where working papers are not available from either of those sources but their existence is identified by a summary list of papers in a Foreign and Commonwealth Office file or in the Minutes, that is noted. As will be apparent from the list below, some anticipated topics (notably K through to Q) were not separately addressed or were addressed in other working paper topics.

Number and title	Minutes reference	Archives reference
Table outlining agreement/disagreement as at 17 August 1979	p 199	
A. The State		
A1 The nature of the State - unitary, federal, decentralised?		Reference in summary list in FCO107/108
A2 The Regions		FCO107/107
A3 Not used		Reference in summary list in FCO107/108
A4 Government Departments		
A5 Tabwemassana, Santo, Nakamal Vila, Draft proposal for administering decentralisation	p 203	
A6 The Region		Reference in summary list in FCO107/108
A6(2) Provincial Administration & Decentralisation (blue)		Reference in summary list in FCO107/108
A7 Decentralisation NHCC No 5		Reference in summary list in FCO107/108
A8 Federal Party Submission - Regions		
A9(2) Decentralisation	p 205	
A9(3) Decentralisation	p 206	FCO107/108
A9(4) Decentralisation		FCO107/109
B. The Head of State		
C. The Executive		
C1. The Executive		Reference in summary list in FCO107/108
C2. The Executive		Reference in summary list in FCO107/108
C3. The Executive: Proposals		Reference in summary list in FCO107/108
C4 The Administration	p 207	FCO107/107
C4(2) Redrafted Article 2 of C4	p 212	

C5 Executive Power		FCO107/107
C6. Constitutional Committee Proposal	p 212 (French)	
C7 The Executive (blue)		FCO107/108
C7(2) Redraft of Article 2 of C7 "Executive"	p 209	FCO107/108
C7(3) Redraft of Article 2 of Document C7 "Executive"	p 209	FCO107/108
C7(4) Redraft of Article 2 of C7 "Executive"		FCO107/108
C7(5) Redraft of Article 2 of C7 "Executive"	p 210	FCO107/108
C7(6) New Article 3 of C7	p 210	FCO107/108
C7(7) New Article 3 of C7	p 211	FCO107/108
C7(8) The Executive		FCO107/109
C7(9) Election of the President of the Republic		FCO107/109
C8 Administration		FCO107/108
C8(2) Redraft of article 7 of C8	p 211 (French)	FCO107/108
D. Legislature		
D1 The Parliament	p 213	FCO107/107
D1(2) Parliament, Redraft of Article 2	p 214	
D1(3) Parliament, Redraft of Article 3		Reference in summary list in FCO107/108
D1(4) Parliament, Redraft of Article 2	p 214	
D1(5) Parliament, Redraft of Article 10 of paper D1	p 215	
D1(6) Parliament, Redraft of Article 2	p 216	
D1(7) Parliament	p 232 (French)	FCO107/108
D1(8) New Article 6 and 6A of D1(7)		FCO107/108
D1(9) New Section (Art 9) of D1(7) (Parliament)	p 233	FCO107/108
D1(10) New Article (Art 9) of D1(7) (Parliament)		FCO107/108
D1(11) New Section 16(3)		FCO107/109
D2 Council of Chiefs		Reference at Minutes 81
E. Judiciary		
E1 Justice		FCO107/107
E1(2) Justice		Reference in summary list in FCO107/108
E1(3) Justice		Reference in summary list in FCO107/108; Minutes 72
E2 Redraft of E1 – based on consensus reached		Reference in summary list in FCO107/108

E2 Justice (blue)	p 233 (French)	FCO107/108
E3 Justice		FCO107/109
Chapter 8 Justice		FCO107/109
F. Amendments to the Constitution		
F1 The Revision of the Constitution		FCO107/107; FCO107/108
F1(2) Amendment of the Constitution	p 235	FCO107/108
G. Fundamental Rights		
G1. National Goals and Basic Principles		Reference in summary list in FCO107/108
G2 Fundamental Rights		FCO107/107
G3. NHCC Fundamental Rights Proposal		Reference in summary list in FCO107/108
G3 Preface	p 236	
G3 Human Rights	p 237 (French)	
G4 Tabwemassana Proposal to the Constitutional Committee, Fundamental Obligations	p 239	
G5 Tabwemassana Proposals to the Constitutional Committee	p 238	
G6 Fundamental Rights, Fundamental Obligations, Enforcement of Fundamental Rights (blue)	p 240	FCO107/108
G7 Tabwemassana preamble	p 242	
G8 Draft Preamble	p 243	FCO107/108
G9 Untitled (Preamble)		FCO107/108
H. Citizenship		
H1 Citizenship		FCO107/107
H1(2) Yash Ghai's Redraft of H1, Articles 1-3		Reference in summary list in FCO107/108; Minutes 95, 96
H2 Professor Zorgbibe, New Hebrides citizenship	p 243	
H3 Constitutional Committee, Citizenship Rules	p 246	
H4 Citizenship (blue)	p 247 (French)	FCO107/108
I. Finance		
J. Land		
J1 The Land		FCO107/107
J1(2) Land		FCO107/108; FCO107/111
J1(3) Tabwemassana, The Land	p 248 (French)	
J2 Land	p 249	
J3 Land	p 250 (French)	
J4 Land	p 250 (French)	
J4(2) Land	p 251	

J4(3) Land	p 252	
J4(4) New Article 4 for Document J4, Redraft of Article 4 of J4		FCO107/108
J4(5) Redraft of Article 4 of J4		FCO107/108
J4(6) New Section 75		FCO107/109
K. The Laws		
L. Electoral Commission		
M. Salary Tribunal		
N. Police		
O. Ombudsman		
P. Official Opposition		
Q. Legal Services		
R. Miscellaneous		
R1 Sovereignty		FCO107/107
R1(2) The State & Sovereignty (blue)		FCO 107/108
R2 Role of the Chiefs	p 252 (French)	
R3 The Leadership Code	p 255	
R3(2) Leadership Code		FCO107/108
R3(3) New Hebrides Council of Churches Submission No 6 Leadership Code	p 258	
R4 National Council of Chiefs (blue)		FCO107/108
R4(2) Council of Chiefs	p 259	
R5 Emergency Measures	p 260 (French)	
Public Emergency	p 262	
R5(3) Public Emergency	p 263	FCO107/108
R6 Transitional Provisions	p 263	
R7 Transitional Provisions	p 265	FCO107/108
R7(2) Transitional Provisions		FCO107/108
R7(3) Transitional Provisions		FCO107/108
R7(4) Transitional Provisions		FCO107/109
Chapter 15 Transitional Provisions		FCO107/109

Index

Index